THE ACTORS

THE SCREENPLAY
WITH AN AFTERWORD BY

CONOR McPHERSON

THE NHB SHOOTING SCRIPTS SERIES

NICK HERN BOOKS
LONDON
www.nickhernbooks.co.uk

The Shooting Script Series

Screenplay copyright © 2003 by Film Four Ltd/Company of Wolves (The Actors) Ltd
Afterword copyright © 2003 Conor McPherson
Front cover image © 2003 Momentum Pictures
Production Stills
Photographer: Tom Collins
Copyright © 2003 Film Four Ltd/Company of Wolves (The Actors) Ltd

The Shooting Script Series was originally devised by Newmarket Press

The Newmarket Shooting Script Series is a registered trademark of Newmarket Press,
a division of Newmarket Publishing & Communications Corporation

This book first published in 2003 as an original paperback by
Nick Hern Books Limited, 14 Larden Road, London W3 7ST

A CIP catalogue record for this book is available from the British Library

ISBN 1 85459 736 1

Typeset by Country Setting, Kingsdown, Kent CT14 8ES
Printed and bound in Great Britain by Hobbs the Printers Ltd,
Totton, Hants. SO40 3YS

THE NHB SHOOTING SCRIPT SERIES
Adaptation
A Beautiful Mind
Erin Brockovich
Gosford Park
The Ice Storm
I Went Down
Saltwater
The Shawshank Redemption
The Truman Show

For information on forthcoming titles, please contact the publishers:
NHB, 14 Larden Road, London W3 7ST

CONTENTS

Conor McPherson

PREFACE

Like every screenplay, the ones I'm involved in anyway, there are marked differences between what you read here and how we do it in the film. A big difference is the role of Mary's monologues. At a point before filming, our financiers said they would like to see more of Mary. I thought it might be a nice idea to see the world of the story through her eyes. So we shot it the way it is scripted here. But when we got to the test screenings, the audience hated her. I couldn't understand why. I thought she was great.

But slowly it dawned on me what was happening. The audience hated her because she was telling them *how to think*. She was saying 'Okay, we've all seen this film. Let's decide what it means . . . ' This was a big mistake. I realise now how pretentious it was. I genuinely thought we'd all think this little kid being grown up and appealing to our innocent good nature was a good idea. Boy was I wrong.

Neil Jordan suggested I shoot her telling the story from her classroom, writing it all down. So I reshot it that way and tried various ways of getting her to talk to us. These things were all written in my normal organised way, on envelopes, the margins of newspapers, etc. I came up with the idea of her saying that none of the story actually happened at the end of the film.

Bigger mistake.

The audience hated the idea that we made them watch this mad film and then told them that none of it was real. It's like the audience's inner child want it to be real somehow. Being told the magic was just an illusion made everybody feel horrible. So I changed it further until everybody was happy and they all liked Mary.

I could go and transcribe what happens in the film for this publication but I thought you might be interested in what I tried (and failed) to make work. So I've left it.

THE ACTORS

screenplay
by
Conor McPherson

X.   EXT. THEATRE DAY

MARY approaches theatre entrance and goes in.

1.   INT. THEATRE DAY

MARY, nine years old, talks to us in a relaxed, grown-up fashion. She is
onstage in a theatre. Around her STAGE HANDS are striking a set. The set
is based on the Nazi Nuremburg rallies. Nobody seems to notice her.

                    MARY
          Everything in moderation. That's
          supposed to be the secret, isn't it? That's
          how you stay out of trouble. But no-one
          seems to be able to do that, do they?
          None of the grown-ups I've met anyway.
          I'm going to be like all of you soon. I'm
          going to grow up. Soon. So I've got to
          tell you all about what happened now.
          If I don't I'll be an adult just like you.
          I won't be here any more. And I won't be
          able to believe we did what we did. Just
          like you probably won't. But I've got to
          give it a go. Before I disappear.

          This is the story of my Uncle Tommy
          and Mr O'Malley and Dolores and
          Barreller. And Mrs Magnani and about
          how everybody got upset. Because they
          were all confused. This is the story
          about the actors.

2.   INT. A THEATRE

It could be day or night. We are presented with a creature on stage. We
have no context.

                    TOM
          'Now is the winter of our discontent
          Made glorious summer by this son of York;
          And all the clouds that lour'd upon our house
          In the deep bosom of the ocean buried.

3

Now are our brows bound with victorious wreaths;
Our bruised arms hung up for monuments;
Our stern alarums changed to merry meetings,
Our dreadful marches to delightful measures.
Grim visag'd war hath smoothed his wrinkled front,
And now instead of mounting barbed steeds
To fright the souls of fearful adversaries.
He capers nimbly in a lady's chamber
To the lascivious pleasings of a lute.'

He begins to limp around, becoming more grotesque, but clown-like.

                    TOM
But I – that am not shap'd for sportive tricks,
Nor made to court an amorous looking glass –
I – that am rudely stamp'd, and want love's majesty
To strut before a wanton ambling nymph
I that am curtail'd of this fair proportion,
Cheated of feature by dissembling nature,
Deform'd, unfinish'd, sent before my time
Into this breathing world scarce half made up . . .

He is interrupted by a tired voice.

                    DIRECTOR
Just say what's on the card will you?

We see the whole situation. This is a school hall. This is a grim audition.
TOM, an actor in his twenties, is on the stage. He's being taped by a
camcorder. The DIRECTOR and ASSISTANTS stand around a table in the
middle of the hall. There are high windows and rain pummels against
them. This is Dublin in the present.

                    TOM
I was told to prepare something.

                    DIRECTOR
If you can just say what's on the card,
please.

TOM is handed a card and a packet of sausages

                    DIRECTOR
Just look into the camera, okay? (To
CAMCORDER GUY.) Okay?

                    CAMCORDER GUY
Hold up the packet.

TOM raises the packet of sausages.

                    DIRECTOR
Higher please. And just what's on the
card. Okay.

4

TOM
(reading card)
'McCullaghs. My, God, that's a right
lump of a sausage.'

DIRECTOR
Could you put a bit more welly in it?

TOM
Welly . . . 'McCullaghs. My God, that's a
right lump of a sausage.'

DIRECTOR
Sell it to me.

TOM
(a bit more gusto)
'McCullaghs . . .'

DIRECTOR
Yeah, come on . . .

TOM
Sorry. I'm just finding it hard to get
worked up about this, you know?

DIRECTOR
Where's your feelings? You're an actor!
Come on . . .

TOM stands there. He stares beyond the room.

TOM
(more gusto. Like a pirate)
McCullaghs!! . . . My God . . . I'm sorry . . .

He picks up his bag and coat. He begins to walk off stage

DIRECTOR
Oh excuse me . . . Didn't mean to offend
you . . . We didn't mean to offend your
sensibilities.

TOM
I'm sorry . . .

DIRECTOR
Next! No more time-wasters, Barry . . .
For Christ's sake. What the fuck was
that about?

TITLE SEQUENCE:

3. INT. CORRIDOR DAY

TOM pushes his way down a corridor which is absolutely jam-packed with ACTORS saying 'McCullaghs. My God, that's a right lump of a sausage.'

4. EXT. STREET DAY

TOM walks down the street in the pouring rain. He is soaked. He passes an electrical shop. Televisions are on in the window. There are appalling performances from daytime TV shows and old B movies. TOM watches their silent posturing for a moment.

5. EXT. TOM'S HOUSE DAY

TOM goes to his house. It's tiny. He opens his door and goes in.

6. INT. BATHROOM DAY

TOM dries his hair with a towel. He looks at himself in the mirror. He hunches over. He moves a little, contorting his face.

7. INT. TOM'S KITCHEN DAY

TOM has a towel around his shoulders. He is cooking the sausages. He is eating them, reading a text of Richard III. We see him become lost in it. In the kitchen are photographs of his niece, MARY, and some of her drawings.

8. INT. TOM'S LIVING ROOM EVENING

TOM puts on his anorak. He takes a bag and checks his things, lozenges, decongestant, script. One or two books by people like Simon Callow and Antony Sher about the craft of acting. On the mantelpiece is the happy mask/sad mask emblem of theatrics. Again more pictures of himself and MARY together. And more of her pictures. And photos of TOM in different parts.

9. INT. HALLWAY/KITCHEN NIGHT

Tom burps loudly. He feels his stomach. That doesn't feel too good. He throws the rest of the McCullaghs' sausages into the bin. As TOM goes out we see that he's left the cooker on.

9A. EXT. THEATRE EVENING

Tom is walking to work

10.   EXT. STAGE DOOR NIGHT

In the rain we see the red neon of Stage Door. TOM approaches the door,
The Stage Door manager holds it open for him.

END OF TITLE SEQUENCE

11.   INT. THEATRE NIGHT

We move from the foyer through some curtains. We can hear a
performance in progress. We see a poster for the show, 'Art ot the State
Theatre presents William Shakespeare's Richard III.' There are production
photos of the CAST mugging around in Nazi uniforms. There is a single
review quotation, doctored to make it look better than 'Anthony O'Malley
is PERFECT-ly adequate as Richard.' We go through to the auditorium and
up towards the stage.

The auditorium is half full. Some people are asleep. A MAN is having a
sneezing fit into a roll of toilet paper. On stage, the formidable figure of
ANTHONY O'MALLEY, late forties, early fifties, plays Richard, Duke of
Gloucester. The production seems to be designed to say something about
the rise of Hitler. Large swastika banners and Third Reich emblems adorn
what looks like the Brandenburg Gate upstage. TOM stands in the wings
waiting to come on, nervously holding a letter. It's Act IV. Sc. iv.

> O'MALLEY
> Where is the power then, to beat him
> back? Where be thy tenants and thy
> followers? Are they now upon the
> western shore? Safe conducting the
> rebels from their ships?

> ACTOR 1
> (playing Derby)
> No, my good lord, my friends are in the
> north.

> O'MALLEY
> Cold friends to me. What do they in the
> north? When they should serve their
> sovereign in the west?

Enter ACTOR 2. TOM gets ready, his cue is coming up. O'MALLEY'S
performance is steadily building to a rage. Everybody is just awful.

> ACTOR 2
> (playing First Messenger; battle dress, wounded, dying)
>   My gracious sovereign now Devonshire,
>   As I by my friends are well advertised,
>   Sir Edward Courtney and the haughty prelate,
>   Bishop of Exeter, his elder brother,
>   With many more confederates are in view.

Enter ACTOR 3. TOM begins saying his lines to himself.

7

                              TOM
                            (quietly)
              'My lord, the army of great Buckingham . . .
              My lord, the army of great Buckingham . . .
              My lord, the army of great Buckingham.'

                             ACTOR 3
      (playing Second Messenger; high-ranking battle dress, wounded, dying)
                In Kent, my liege, the Guildfords are in arms;
                And every hour more competitors
                Flock to the rebels, and their power grows strong.

      Here's TOM's big moment. Enter 'Messenger Three'.

                              TOM
              My lord, the army of great Buckingham –

      O'MALLEY lands a horrible slap on the side of TOM's head.

                            O'MALLEY
              Out on you owls! Nothing but songs of death?

      TOM winces away and O'MALLEY goes to kick him up the arse, but sort of
      ruptures himself. He continues his lines, hobbling around a little bit,
      clutching his groin, the wind gone out of his sails.

                            O'MALLEY
              There, take thou that till . . . thou . . . bring . . .
              better news.

12.   INT. DRESSING ROOM NIGHT

      TOM and O'MALLEY share a cramped dressing room. TOM helps
      O'MALLEY to take off his hump. O'MALLEY talks to his agent on his
      mobile phone. TOM hangs O'MALLEY's costume up for him.

                            O'MALLEY
                  I know, Arthur. But it's soul destroying.
                  Have you seen it? Don't. And maybe it
                  wouldn't be so bad if some of these
                  fucking bastards could act. I know, I
                  know. But the point is, it's not worth it.
                  Two hundred and twenty quid to debase
                  myself like this, Arthur. There has to be
                  something else on the horizon. Nothing?
                  Really? Jesus, because we're fucking
                  dying here every night. I know. No, I'm
                  good, I'm fine. Just there's so many
                  talentless spare pricks all over the
                  fucking stage, Arthur. I know. Okay. But
                  the first sign of anything, get on to me,
                  will you? I'm bollocksed with my rent.

I'm out on my ear, you know that? Those
sausage bastards? They don't know
what they're looking for. Okay. Okay.
Bye. Bye Arthur.

He turns off the phone and talks to TOM.

> O'MALLEY
> I need a new agent.

> TOM
> I need an agent, full stop.

> O'MALLEY
> Arthur would probably take you on. But
> he's useless. I need someone who can . . .
> I need to do a big film or something.
> Look at this.

He holds up a newspaper with a picture of a castle and a headline, 'Far
And Away II, Cruise to stay at exclusive Tubbetstown Castle.'

> O'MALLEY
> This is how an actor should be treated.
> Tubbetstown Castle. Ten grand a night.
> The whole place to yourself. That's my
> dream. I'm not fucking around. (Fiddling
> with his balls.) I think I might have
> ruptured myself.

> TOM
> What were you doing? Throwing the
> boot into me?

> O'MALLEY
> I was going for it! That's what I was
> doing.

> TOM
> I swear to God I saw stars. You hit me
> harder every night.

> O'MALLEY
> I'm trying to make a connection. Get a
> response.

> TOM
> I'm doing my best.

> O'MALLEY
> You probably are.

O'MALLEY fills a flask from the boiling dressing-room kettle.

                    O'MALLEY
          It, it, it . . . all comes down to 'To be or
          not to be.' It's not just Hamlet's
          dilemma. It's the actor's dilemma. Tom.
          You need to decide.

                    TOM
          I think it's fucking 'not to be' in my case.

O'MALLEY regards himself in the mirror.

                    O'MALLEY
          One should never give up hope. Am I
          too old, Tom?

                    TOM
          For what?

                    O'MALLEY
          For Hamlet?

                    TOM
          To play Hamlet himself?

                    O'MALLEY
          Yes.

                    TOM
          In fairness, if I said yes, we'd both be
          deluding ourselves.

                    O'MALLEY
          I would have loved to play Hamlet. But
          . . . but . . . just the vowels. Why didn't
          anyone go with me on that, Tom?

                    TOM
          Because it's a ludicrous idea?

                    O'MALLEY
          Each character vocally crippled. 'Oo cc
          aw am, oo

TOM laughs . . . O'MALLEY puts the lid on his flask.

                    O'MALLEY
          Come on, I'll buy you a pint.

13.   EXT. STREET NIGHT AND SECOND HAND BOOKSHOP

TOM and O'MALLEY walk along, chatting. They stop outside a second
hand bookshop. O'MALLEY carries a bag full of books.

                    O'MALLEY
          Confidence is all about character. Being

                    10

comfortable in it. Losing yourself. You
need a character, what is it?

> TOM

I'm a . . . pall bearer and a messenger.

> O'MALLEY

I need characters, not messengers.

> TOM

I need . . . a message.

> O'MALLEY

A message. You're a character with a
message for me. But who is he? Who
has this message? What does he care
about? Is he in love? How did he sleep
last night? Does he simply want to
return to the bosom of his family? Or
does he want to fight the world? Give us
your lines there.

> TOM

My lord the army of great Buckingham . . .

O'MALLEY slaps him on cue.

14.   INT. SECONDHAND BOOKSHOP

The BOOKSELLER looks through O'MALLEY'S bag of books. TOM and
O'MALLEY are leafing through playscripts. They continue their discussion,

> TOM

He . . .

> O'MALLEY

Yes.

> TOM

Could have a bad . . .

> O'MALLEY

Yes.

> TOM
> (struggling)

Stammer.

> O'MALLEY

Well, no. Because then you'd slow down
my flow. My rhythm. You'd . . .

> TOM

Yes.

                    O'MALLEY

        Stop my juice.

                    TOM

        He could . . . just before he gives his
        message, he could inadvertently,
        because of nerves, make a . . . weird . . .
        honking sound.

                    O'MALLEY

        You're becoming foolish.

                    TOM

        Just no good.

The BOOKSELLER looks at them.

                    BOOKSELLER

        I'll give you a fiver.

O'MALLEY reluctantly nods. The BOOKSELLER opens the till.

15.   INT. AULDFELLAS' BAR NIGHT

This is a quiet little auldfellas' bar. A clock ticks loudly and hollowly. An
OLD MAN reads a newspaper. The BARMAN reads a paperback, 'A
Bluffer's Guide to . . . ' TOM and O'MALLEY chat morosely over pints of
stout.

                    O'MALLEY

        Who got you this job?

                    TOM

        You did.

                    O'MALLEY

        And would I have moved mountains to
        get it for you, if you were no good?

                    TOM

        I don't know. You like having me around.
        Help you with your lines. Take off your
        hump. Rub your shoulder. Which I have
        to say, I don't love actually.

                    O'MALLEY

        You see. I've seen something.

                    TOM

        Where?

                    O'MALLEY

        In you. And I have a proposition.

                     12

                                TOM
What . . . is it?

                              O'MALLEY
Finish your drink. We'll go somewhere a
little more . . . private . . .

                                TOM
You're not gay or anything like that. are
you, 'cause I'm not, like.

                              O'MALLEY
I can assure you that I'm not. But it's
irrelevant. The proposition concerns
some money. And a degree of acting.

TOM shudders.

                              O'MALLEY
Are you alright?

                                TOM
Someone just walked over my grave.

16.   EXT. O'MALLEY'S HOUSE NIGHT

This is a large house in a posh suburb. There's a For Rent sign in the
garden.

                              O'MALLEY
You've never been here.

                                TOM
No.

                              O'MALLEY
                           (opening locks)
Moved in in my glorious past. Voiceovers, American TV. But it's falling apart
now and I can't afford the rent. I'm being
kicked out. Have to get an apartment . . .
or a little flat or . . . a bedsit or something.

17.   INT. O'MALLEY'S HOUSE NIGHT

TOM and O'MALLEY come into O'MALLEY'S hallway. It's a spacious
house, but everything looks run down and dishevelled. It looks like it
needs to be painted and repaired. TOM looks around, surprised at the
size, but also the wreckedness. All around are pictures of O'MALLEY from
productions in younger days

                              O'MALLEY
Voiceovers. That's where the money is.

                    TOM
          I've never had that sort of voice.

                  O'MALLEY
          You never trained.

                    TOM
          Well, I always felt I was always more . . .

                  O'MALLEY
          What.

                    TOM
          Method.

                  O'MALLEY
          Pih. No. Leave your coat on. There's no
          heat.

18. INT. DRAWING ROOM NIGHT

    Again a big room but not much in it, except for photos and memorabilia of
    O'MALLEY'S 'glorious past.' There's bright moonlight and the lads play
    chess, illuminated by candles. Perhaps O'MALLEY lights the fire.
    O'MALLEY pours hot water from the flask into little cups, making tea.
    They clink the cups together.

                    TOM
          So what's this . . . proposition?

                  O'MALLEY
          Well it's a little complex. You'll agree
          with me, acting is not real.

                    TOM
          . . . Yeah . . .

                  O'MALLEY
          Because nothing's really at stake. We're
          just pretending that it is.

                    TOM
                 (affirmative)
          Mmmhmm.

                  O'MALLEY
          But what if something were at stake? I
          mean really at stake. Like life or, death.
          Or money.

                    TOM
          Well, that's real life.

                  O'MALLEY
          Well my proposition is to . . . blur the
          difference.

                      14

TOM

I'm not with you.

O'MALLEY

For the last few weeks, I've been
frequenting a very very rough pub down
the docks.

TOM

What . . . with like . . . sailors?

O'MALLEY

I've been seeking out bad company. For
research. To play Richard I felt I should
meet some real . . . villains.

TOM

Villains?

O'MALLEY

The real thing. To help my performance.
The cutting edge. Lowlifes. The . . .
Godforsaken.

TOM

What, like gangsters or . . .

O'MALLEY

Well, men who operate outside the law.

TOM

And you talk to them?

O'MALLEY

Well, one, in particular.

TOM

And you tell him what you do for a
living?

O'MALLEY

Oh yeah. It . . . flatters him. That he's
being somehow . . . observed. You see,
he's vain, I suppose. He likes it.

TOM

What kind of criminal is he?

O'MALLEY

I get the impression that he's into . . .
many . . . different things.

TOM

Is he . . . violent?

O'MALLEY

One would have to assume that he's . . .
had his moments.

TOM

I think you should watch yourself.

O'MALLEY

Well . . . This is where we come to the . . .
proposition.

TOM

(incredulous tone of 'Have you lost your fucking mind?')
It's to do with this guy?

O'MALLEY

I need you to hear me out.

TOM

(again tone of 'You're a loolah')
For entertainment value . . . I'll listen.

O'MALLEY

You may change your tune. (Warming to
his subject.)

O'MALLEY

As far as I can tell, there's a certain
party owed money by another certain
party and neither party have ever . . .
met. They've never met each other.

TOM

One party owes the other party money.

O'MALLEY

Yes. But they've never met. Now if
someone, let's say someone sitting not a
million miles away from my good self
were to pretend, you see? Pretend that
he were the party to whom money is
owed. If he were to pull this off he could
collect the money.

TOM

If you're serious, you're gone. You've lost
your mind. You know that.

O'MALLEY

Au contraire my gallant compadre. And
you're the man to do it. You're the man
to do . . . the acting.

TOM

Acting . . . I can't act! I'm shit.

16

O'MALLEY

Exactly why this exercise will be invaluable training. Because something is at stake. You've got to formulate all the aspects of your character and never let your facade drop. Manage this and you'll never look back. And you and I, we'll split the proceeds, and be happy men.

TOM

(making a chess move)

Oh I love this, you know, I put my fucking head on the block and you get the money. If your plan is so brilliant, why don't you use your considerable acting skills and do it yourself?

O'MALLEY

I'm too well known. And as I say I've been meeting this man regularly. I could never pass myself off as somebody else.

TOM

You're saying I'm a better actor . . .

O'MALLEY

I'm saying you have the advantage of . . .

TOM

Yes?

O'MALLEY

Anonymity.

TOM

I see.

O'MALLEY

It's a lot of money Tom. And you know this Richard can't last more than another week or two.

TOM

It's always bleak.

O'MALLEY

Well, not any more. Let's talk details.

TOM

I don't want to hear any more Tony. It's late and you're a nutbag.

19. INT. HALLWAY NIGHT

O'MALLEY sees TOM out.

> O'MALLEY
> Tell me you'll think about it.

> TOM
> No.

TOM walks off. O'MALLEY calls after him. He holds up the newspaper with the picture of Tubbetstown Castle.

> O'MALLEY
> Tubbetstown Castle awaits! For men of
> means . . .

> TOM
> You're ridiculous.

> O'MALLEY
> Sleep on it then. 'Come Sleep! The balm
> of woe. The certain knot of peace. The
> poor man's fortune. And the prisoner's
> release.'

20. EXT. STREET NIGHT

TOM walks home down a street in an old suburb. He crosses the road.

21. INT. FISH AND CHIP SHOP NIGHT

TOM waits for an assistant, ANGELO, to dish up his chips into a bag. TOM is the only customer. He is counting out change, trying to see if he has enough.

> TOM
> Hey, Angelo. You ever thought about
> getting rich?

> ANGELO
> I don't know. You're rich, aren't you?

> TOM
> No.

> ANGELO
> Does the acting not pay, no?

> TOM
> Not if you're completely shit, you tell me
> how to get rich, will you?

                    ANGELO
          Mm. I suppose there's the easy way and
          there's the hard way.

                    TOM
          What's the hard way?

                    ANGELO
          This.

TOM watches ANGELO scoop a wadge of greasy chips into a bag.

                    TOM
          And what's the easy way?

                    ANGELO
          Steal it.

                    TOM
          Steal it.

                    ANGELO
          Steal it. Only problem though, stealing's
          wrong.

ANGELO plonks the bag of chips on the counter,

                    ANGELO
          Pound, please, Tom.

                    TOM
              (awkward pause)
          Eh. I don't think I have quite enough.

21A.   EXT. FISH AND CHIP SHOP NIGHT

       TOM exits chip shop.

22.   EXT. TOM'S ROAD

       TOM walks along, eating his chips. He speaks to himself with his mouth
       full. Mulling.

                    TOM
          A certain party. A certain party owed
          money by . . . another party . . . neither
          party having ever met. Neither party
          having ever met.

He stops, staring straight ahead, amber light plays about his face. His
mouth falls open, and chips fall out.

                    TOM
          Oh . . . fuck.

                          19

TOM's little house is ablaze. FIREMEN battle it, but it looks as though the house won't ever be habitable again. TOM stumbles towards the firemen. He stands beside the CHIEF, still automatically eating his chips, mechanically chewing.

                    TOM
          What happened?

                    CHIEF
          Your house?

                    TOM
          Yeah.

A FIREMAN comes over and hands the CHIEF a smouldering pan with charred sausages in it.

                    CHIEF
          This your tea?

TOM looks away in exasperation.

                    CHIEF
          You left the gas on. Is there someone
          you can phone?

The CHIEF hands TOM his phone.

                    TOM
          I'll call my sister.

23.   EXT. / INT. FRONT DOOR TOM'S SISTER'S HOUSE NIGHT

TOM'S sister, RITA opens the door to a forlorn looking TOM, who holds a plastic bag with a few belongings he's managed to salvage. She is in her pyjamas. She's knackered. She hugs him and brings him in.

24.   INT. RITA'S LANDING NIGHT

TOM and RITA pause at a door and quietly look inside where a little girl of nine or so sleeps peacefully. RITA shushes TOM with her finger.

A man's voice, off, calls out in a cockney accent, from another bedroom.

                    CLIVE
                   (off)
          Rita? Are you coming to bed?

                    TOM
          Who's that?

                    RITA
          Clive. He's English.

TOM nods, knowingly, patiently.

                              RITA
          Don't start.

                              CLIVE
                              (off)
          Rita? The hedgehog is going back into
          his shell.

                              RITA
          I'll be in a minute.

25.   INT. SPARE BEDROOM NIGHT

       The door opens and RITA turns on the light. She leads TOM in. He sits on
       the bed opposite a mirror.

                              RITA
          See you in the morning.
                              TOM
          Okay.

       RITA leaves. TOM delves into his plastic bag and pulls out his charred
       happy mask/sad mask ornament. He places it beside his bed. From the
       room next door he hears Clive.

                              CLIVE
                              (off)
          'Allo my darling.

       TOM sees himself in the mirror. He speaks low, mimicking CLIVE, a flick
       of the head.

                              TOM
          'Allo Darling. 'Allo my love. 'Allo.

       He raises his eyebrows. An expression of `Not bad.' He lies back on the
       bed. He stares up at the ceiling.

26.   INT. RITA'S KITCHEN MORNING

       There's a bit of bustle as RITA, CLIVE and MARY prepare for work and
       school. RITA wears a uniform which suggests she's a waitress. MARY is
       ignoring her breakfast, drawing a picture. CLIVE is older than RITA. He
       wears incredibly thick-lensed glasses. He wears a brash suit. He is
       stooping in front of a little mirror, strategically trying to conceal his
       balding scalp. He is covered in jewellery. A piece of toast hangs limply
       from his mouth and he tries to fix a collar pin.

                              CLIVE
                              (mouth full)
          Jiss boodying. Ooks grea' uh fey,
          finickity.

                               21

                         RITA
          Mary, love, eat your breakfast. I'm going
          to be late.

TOM comes in.

                         RITA
          Clive, this is my brother, Tommy.

                         CLIVE
                    (sympathetically)
          Hello, mate. How you doing, alright?

                         TOM
          I'm okay.

                         CLIVE
          I know . . . Still, though, eh?

                         TOM
          Mmm.

MARY continues to draw. She chuckles a little whenever CLIVE says
anything.

                         CLIVE
          Rita tells me you act.

                         MARY
          Great actor. Great actor.

TOM looks at MARY as though she always bewilders him.

                         RITA
          He's the black sheep.

                         MARY
          He's my favourite.

                         CLIVE
          Favourite? Favourite what?

                         MARY
          Just my favourite, Clive. My favourite
          person.

                         RITA
          This pair are always in cahoots.

                         CLIVE
          Oh really? I'm in sales, Tom. Imports
          and sales.

                         TOM
          How's business?

CLIVE

Tom, I'll tell you the truth. It's always a
little slow this time of the year. You've
got to chase every single farthing and
groat they owe you. They'll all disappear
into the woodwork. Like flies. Torn, like
bees.

TOM

O . . . kay.

RITA

Mary, come on. You're going to make me
late.

MARY

Tommy can bring me.

CLIVE

I've got to push off myself. Like a
beekeeper.

MARY
(still just drawing)
Ah don't go, Clive, you're great craic.

TOM looks at MARY and laughs at her. She looks up for the first time and
chuckles conspiratorially.

CLIVE

Get cracking . . .

27.   EXT. ON THE WAY TO SCHOOL MORNING

TOM and MARY stroll along a leafy avenue. TOM carries MARY'S
schoolbag. She is deep in thought. Perhaps her arms are folded in
consternation . . .

MARY
. . . A certain party owed money by
another certain party. And neither party
has ever met each other. A tantalising
proposition, Uncle Tommy. Potentially
very lucrative.

TOM

And if someone were to . . . you know?

MARY

Pass themselves off as the party to
whom money is owed . . . someone with
great skill. An actor perhaps. Perhaps an
actor whose house burned down?

23

28.   EXT. OUTSIDE MARY'S SCHOOL GATES DAY

CHILDREN play in the yard. TOM and MARY pause at the gate.

> TOM
> Actors need characters, Mary. Precisely
> my weak point, you know?

> MARY
> (cockney)
> Well perhaps. This character could be . . .
> in a motor. Know wot I mean, dawlin?

> TOM
> (laughs)
> That's pretty good. (Cockney.) In a
> motor. A character in a motor.

He hunkers down, giving her her schoolbag.

> MARY
> I think you could do it. I think you could
> do anything you wanted.

> TOM
> No, Mary.

> MARY
> If you don't believe in yourself you'll
> never convince anyone that you're not
> you.

> TOM
> What?

> MARY
> Tommy. Trust me.

> TOM
> Mary. You're nine.

> MARY
> Then why are you telling me about it?

> TOM
> Because. Because you're weird and
> clever and you know too much. It's like
> you were born like a grown up person or
> something.

> MARY
> I was born ancient, Tommy.

                    TOM
          Don't say that. Don't say things like that.
          It's really creepy, you know? I mean
          really.

MARY sighs and starts to walk off,

                    TOM
          Where are you going?

                    MARY
          Come on, we have to get you ready.

                    TOM
          You have to go to school!

                    MARY
          I don't need it.

                    TOM
          Mary! I can't do characters. I can't act!

She turns. She stamps her foot in exasperation.

                    MARY
          Let's just try!

TOM looks at the school and at the receding figure of MARY. He resigns
himself and follows MARY.

29.   INT. RITA'S BEDROOM DAY

MARY is reaching into the wardrobe.

                    MARY
          Come on, eejit head, I can't reach.

                    TOM
          Yeah, and Clive won't miss his clothes.

                    MARY
          Clive is very, very thick, Tom.

                    TOM
          But that's like really thick.

                    MARY
          He is. He's really thick.

                    TOM
               (unquestioning)
          Okay.

TOM reaches into the wardrobe.

                       25

30.   INT. LIVING ROOM DAY

TOM stands in Clive's gear. Clive's taste is both flamboyant and
ill-judged. MARY stands looking at him. She holds her lunchbox. They
both eat her sandwiches.

                    TOM
        Two words. A bit much.

                    MARY
        One word. Not enough.

31.   INT. SAME DAY

TOM and MARY sit in front of a mirror. MARY now has a scarf around her
head like a pirate. They have a box of jewellery in front of them. They are
both extremely bejewelled. MARY is putting gel in TOM'S hair, slicking it
back.

                    MARY
        More rings.

                    TOM
        Any more rings and my fingers'll fall off.
        Mary.

                    MARY
                (laughing)
        No they won't! Come on.

She places a large mounted sovereign on his little finger.

                    TOM
        Are we married now?

                    MARY
        Tom, you don't embarrass me. You
        embarrass yourself.

32.   INT. SAME DAY

TOM sits on the sofa. MARY places an unbelievably thick pair of
spectacles on him. His eyes look huge. He blinks. The effect is gruesome.

                    TOM
        I can't see.

                    MARY
                (starts jumping up and down on the sofa)
        Tommy, anyone wearing those glasses
        is for real.

26

33.   INT. SAME DAY

MARY sits at one end of the room at a table with a few objects on it, a
newspaper, a pack of cigarettes, a bottle of wine and a glass, a knife and
fork. TOM stands at the other end of the room.

> MARY
> Okay, come over here and sit down.

TOM starts towards her. He has developed a shrugging motion and a way
of stretching his head to the side as though his collar is too tight. He
tumbles over a chair.

34.   INT. SAME DAY

TOM now sits at the table opposite MARY.

> MARY
> Would you like a drink, Clive?

> TOM
> (cockney)
> A drink would be smashing!

> MARY
> Well, I'm not your servant.

TOM fumbles for and finds the wine and the glass. He holds the glass and
pours the wine, missing the glass, all over the floor.

> MARY
> Would you like a cigarette? Please help
> yourself.

Again TOM fumbles around and finds the fags. He puts one in his mouth,
eventually, filter sticking out, a look of nonchalant devil-may-care ease on
his face. He can't light the cigarette with the lighter. He keeps trying. He
looks like a complete headcase.

> MARY
> You can't trust your eyes.

> TOM
> Well then what can I trust?

> MARY
> Use the force.

> TOM
> What force?

> MARY
> Force of habit.

27

35.   INT. SAME DAY

TOM sits in a chair. He is blindfolded. He holds an orange. He tosses it into the air. He tries to catch it. He fails.

36.   INT. SAME DAY

He throws an apple and tries to catch it. He fails.

37.   INT. SAME DAY

TV remote control. He fails.

38.   INT. SAME DAY

A bunch of keys. He fails.

39.   INT. SAME DAY

A little teddy bear. He fails.

40.   INT. SAME DAY

An orange. He catches it. MARY throws another one. He catches it.

41.   INT. SAME DAY

A shot of the glass. The wine is poured in perfectly by TOM'S ring-bedecked hand. We hear MARY'S voice.

                    MARY
          You do all these things every day. You
          don't need to look. Trust yourself. It's
          only when you start thinking that you
          stop being able to do stuff. If you try
          walking, I mean, actually, putting one
          foot in front of the other, you're going to
          fall. If you tried speaking no one would
          understand you. If you tried consciously
          breathing all the time, you'd die! You
          can't control your heart. You're heart
          won't let you.

We see the lighter struck perfectly and follow it up the cigarette, bang on target.

                    MARY
          And you're an actor. You should be more
          self aware than everybody else. See?

The lighter is slipped into a pocket, as though he wears this jacket every day. We see TOM'S face as he smokes. His eyes really are massive.

28

TOM

If I don't walk under a bus first.

MARY

You'll be fine. I know it's going to work.

TOM takes off the glasses and rubs his eyes.

MARY

Really. Really.

She begins to applaud him. Which becomes . . .

42.   INT. THEATRE NIGHT

A weak round of applause from a half-full theatre. The cast of Richard III
are taking, their curtain call. O'MALLEY behaves as though he's just
received an Olivier award.

O'MALLEY

Thank you. No. Thank you. Please. My
colleagues.

He gestures towards the rest of the cast, some of whom shake their heads
in embarrassment. The audience are beginning to file out. The house
lights are coming on, O'MALLEY still bows. Finally, mercifully, the curtain
agonisingly descends.

43.   INT. BACKSTAGE NIGHT

O'MALLEY joins TOM in the wings. The STAGE MANAGER is handing out
wage packets.

O'MALLEY

Ungrateful bastards. What the fuck am I
breaking my arse for every night? None
of the stupid fucking knackers
understand any of it anyway.

TOM

I barely understand it.

The STAGE MANAGER hands them their wage packets.

STAGE MANAGER

There you go lads. Enjoy it. Be all over
soon.

O'MALLEY

Jesus. Put me out of my misery.

44.   INT. DRESSING ROOM NIGHT

TOM helps O'MALLEY take his hump off.

O'MALLEY

The main pleasure of this play, I
conclude, is the embodiment of pure
unmotivated evil.

TOM

Listen . . .

O'MALLEY

I run like a knife through the butter that
is the cast of other characters.

TOM

I was thinking. With the house burned
down. And no insurance, And generally
being completely fucked.

O'MALLEY

Each step I make is so outrageous as to
brook no opposition.

TOM

This proposition. We spoke about. It
mightn't in fact, upon sober reflection,
be the most stupid direction an actor
could take. At this point.

O'MALLEY

And yet. I'm such a bundle of schemes
and contradictions, I soar through the
text as one might peruse a racing
form.(Sudden dismay.) What happened
to us?

TOM

The certain party that doesn't know the
other certain party.

O'MALLEY stops wallowing in self-intrigue and looks at TOM in the
mirror.

TOM

I want to do it.

O'MALLEY

My boy . . .

45.   INT. AULDFELLAS' BAR NIGHT

They are back in their favourite little auldfellas' bar. One or two OLD MEN.
The BARMAN reads a new, different 'Bluffer's Guide to . . . ' TOM and
O'MALLEY are hunched conspiratorially over their pints.

                    O'MALLEY
You know the Cock and Weathervane.

                    TOM
Goodnight . . .

                    O'MALLEY
Our certain party holds court there every
night.

                    TOM
That place is bedlam.

                    O'MALLEY
They know me. I tend to be with this
certain party.

                    TOM
Who is . . . ?

                    O'MALLEY
Barreller.

                    TOM
Barreller what?

                    O'MALLEY
I know him only as Barreller.

                    TOM
And he's of the . . . criminal fraternity.

                    O'MALLEY
Very much so.

                    TOM
And the other certain party.

                    O'MALLEY
An English outfit.

                    TOM
Ah ha . . .

                    O'MALLEY
What does that mean?

                    TOM
(tone of 'This might work out okay')
It means ah ha ha hah . . .

46.   INT. PHONE BOOTH IN AULDFELLAS' PUB NIGHT

TOM and O'MALLEY are squashed into the little booth. TOM is dialling a
number from the tattered directory. He speaks to O'MALLEY,

                     31

                         TOM
            I . . . represent a certain party.

                       O'MALLEY
            Absolutely. You are here to do a job.

                         TOM
            My name is Clive.

                       O'MALLEY
            If it makes you comfortable.

                         TOM
            Anything else I should know?

                       O'MALLEY
            These people are tough, Clive.

                         TOM
            So a little threat. Behind a little veil . . .

                       O'MALLEY
            Nothing specific.

                         TOM
            The party I represent will be most
            displeased if . . .

                       O'MALLEY
            You don't want things to become
            unpleasant.

                         TOM
            However.

                       O'MALLEY
            Absolutely. Business after all. As usual.

                         TOM
            It's ringing.

        We hear the ringing tone.

46A. EXT. COCK AND WEATHERVANE NIGHT.

        The Bouncers throw a guy out of the pub and there's a scuffle. We go in.
        We discover BARRELLER.

        RETURN TO

46B.   INT. PHONE BOOTH IN AULDFELLAS' PUB NIGHT

                       O'MALLEY
                    (patting Tom's stomach)
        Breathe from here.

                          32

VOICE ON PHONE

Baltic.

TOM
(cockney)

Yes. Barreller please.

O'MALLEY gives his accent an approving thumbs up. He hears
BARRELLER down the phone. Broad Dublin accent.

BARRELLER

Barreller.

TOM

Barreller. I'll come straight to the point.
I represent a certain party.

BARRELLER

Yeah?

TOM

To whom you owe a certain amount of
money.

BARRELLER

From over the water?

TOM

Well as it happens, I've just arrived in
your fair city.

BARRELLER

For your money?!

TOM

The very thing.

BARRELLER

I wasn't expecting you. I was going to
send it over.

TOM

I've saved you the bother.

BARRELLER

This is a lot of money. I'll need a couple
of days.

TOM

I'm leaving tomorrow.

BARRELLER

Ah, now here, mister.

                          TOM
              Clive. You can call me Clive.

                        BARRELLER
              Clive. I think you're being unreasonable
              to me.

                          TOM
              And I believe that a debt is a debt.

                        BARRELLER
              I never renege on a deal. But tomorrow
              is so soon.

                          TOM
              The party I represent will be satisfied
              with nothing less than payment in full.
              And although I am a reasonable man,
              the party I represent is, I'm afraid, vice
              versa.

                        BARRELLER
              There's no need for this to get messy.

                          TOM
              I agree. Tomorrow. The Shelbourne. At
              five.

                        BARRELLER
              I can't . . .

TOM hangs up. O'MALLEY is impressed.

                        O'MALLEY
              Textbook.

                          TOM
                (looking at his hand shaking violently)
              It's . . . promising.

47.   INT. BAR IN THE SHELBOURNE HOTEL DAY

We discover TOM sitting, dressed as CLIVE, legs crossed, smoking a
cheroot. He's added a thick moustache to the disguise. He has a magazine
on his lap. He is glancing over the top of his glasses at prospective
Barrellers. He doesn't see one. He looks at his watch. It is five twenty.
He tips his ash nervously, looking around. Then at the entrance to the
bar a PORTER points him out to a small group of people. BARRELLER is
in his fifties and casually dressed. With him are two young MEN in their
twenties and a beautiful young WOMAN. They approach TOM. He pushes
his glasses into place. BARRELLER is sweating. He wipes himself with a
handkerchief, he carries a briefcase.

                    BARRELLER
              (shaking hand with TOM)
          Never again.

                       TOM
          You're very late. I was beginning to
          worry.

They sit down.

                    BARRELLER
          We went to the dog track by mistake.
          Shelbourne Park, you know?

                       TOM
          I'm not familiar with it, no.

                    BARRELLER
          And then the traffic was only fucking
          vicious. These are my sons, Ronnie and
          Lesley.

TOM shakes their hands. Holding his hand for them to reach, so he
doesn't have to find them.

                       TOM
          Clive. From London.

                    BARRELLER
          And this is my daughter, Dolores.

From TOM'S POV she is a blurry figure TOM looks at her over his glasses.
She becomes clear. She is very attractive.

                       TOM
          Charmed, I'm sure.

His hand lingers on hers, genuinely taken with her beauty.

                    BARRELLER
          I had a nightmare raising this.

He hands the suitcase to DOLORES. She passes it on to TOM.

                       TOM
          What you have to realise is that my
          client, bless his heart, appreciates all
          effort in extremis. He will be deeply
          impressed.

                    BARRELLER
          Is he always this hard to please?

                       TOM
          He thrives on . . . rage. Just as you and

                       35

I need to eat and sleep he needs to be
full of . . . anger.

                    BARRELLER
That's not brilliant.

                    TOM
No. But it gets results.

TOM snaps open the catches on the briefcase.

                    BARRELLER
Jesus, man. Don't open it in here.

                    TOM
Don't be nervous. I'm just.

He opens it a little. He is taken aback at the amount of money.

                    BARRELLER
It's all there. Fifty thou.

                    DOLORES
                    (coldly)
I counted it.

                    TOM
Well, aren't you a treasure. My client will
be very pleased.

                    BARRELLER
And we're clear now?

                    TOM
You're free as a bird Mr Barreller. Until
you next decide to do some business
with us.

                    BARRELLER
Hoho, no next time. No way. I'm totally
legitimate from now on, Clive. I can't be
up to this any more. Too old.

                    TOM
You're saying my client isn't legitimate?

                    BARRELLER
No. Just. I have to leave something
stable for the boys. Something above
board. Neither of them are brilliant, you
know? Lesley's not all there, you know?
Are you Lesley.

                    LESLEY
No, I'm not, no.

36

TOM

I . . . see.

BARRELLER

And Ronnie's deaf in one ear. Ronnie.

RONNIE

What?

TOM

How unfortunate. (To DOLORES.) You, I
trust are in the whole of your health?

BARRELLER
(another burden)
She wants to get into the acting!

TOM

Oh really?

DOLORES
(embarrassed)
We know an actor, comes into the Baltic.
Anthony O'Malley. (Forceful, at
BARRELLER.) He's going to help me.
Get training.

BARRELLER
('Have you ever heard anything as ridiculous?')
Get training, you know?

TOM

Oh, is he, now?

BARRELLER

Do you know him?

TOM

Never heard of him.

A WAITER arrives with a tray of flaming sambucas.

TOM

Ah, thank you.

BARRELLER

What are these?

TOM

A drink to no hard feelings. Flaming
sambucas. Blow it out first Lesley.

RONNIE

What?

                              TOM
                 Well this was very easy.

TOM and DOLORES blow theirs out. The others view the drink
suspiciously and then finally blow them out and drink it. None of them
like it. But DOLORES does.

                            DOLORES
                 That's really nice.

TOM clinks glasses with her. BARRELLER hands her his.

                           BARRELLER
                 Have mine. Here, Clive, I'll take you for
                 a real drink. You have to have a pint in
                 the Baltic. I have a share in it. Meet
                 some real Dubs. Not this bollocks.

                             CLIVE
                 Well. I don't know. I do have to catch a
                 plane.

TOM is smitten by DOLORES. He's fighting his better judgement.

48.   INT. BARRELLER'S VAN DAY

BARRELLER, TOM and DOLORES sit in the front of BARRELLER'S place.
RONNIE and LESLEY are in the back with a load of car parts. They drive
down the Quays. The traffic is heavy.

                           BARRELLER
                 Fuck this.

BARRELLER reaches into the glove compartment. He pulls out a police
blue light and sticks it on the roof. He activates a siren and cars pull over
to let them through.

                           BARRELLER
                 So how's business with you, Clive? In
                 general.

                              TOM
                 Barreller, I'll tell you the truth. It's
                 always a little slow this time of the year.
                 You've got to chase every single farthing
                 and groat they owe you. They'll all
                 disappear into the woodwork. Like flies,
                 Barreller, like bees.

                           BARRELLER
                 I wasn't disappearing anywhere, Clive.

                              TOM
                 I know. Barreller. But one has to follow

                               38

orders, eh? Plus I get to have a little trip
to Dublin.

He smiles at DOLORES.

> DOLORES
> What do you mean, people disappear
> like bees?

> TOM
> I . . . don't know.

> BARRELLER
> East End expression, Clive?

> TOM
> It . . . must be. Yeah.

He looks out the window. His expression is one of 'What the fuck am I
doing?'

49.   INT. THE COCK AND WEATHERVANE EARLY EVENING

The pub is full of hardcases. A Karaoke machine is set up. A headbanger
sings a song. TOM sits rather uncomfortably with BARRELLER and
DOLORES. They shout above the din.

> BARRELLER
> So what's Mr Magnani like?

> TOM
> Who?

> BARRELLER
> Your boss, what's he like?

> TOM
> Oh! (Pronouncing it differently.) Mr
> Magnanay?

> BARRELLER
> Yeah. Mr Magananny, I've never met
> him.

> TOM
> (struggling)
> Mmm. Hard to say. I've only met him
> once or twice. Mr Magnenyey is quite a
> recluse.

> BARRELLER
> A second hand car dealer who's a
> recluse?

39

TOM
Second . . . hand . . . car . . . dealer.

A welcome tray of pints of stout arrive. TOM picks one up and drinks it all.
BARRELLER and DOLORES look a little concerned.

BARRELLER
. . . Eh . . . Cheers . . .

TOM
Well. He eh, he leaves the day to day
running of his empire to his trusted . . .
associates. He himself, in the . . .
autumn of his years, surrounds himself
with grandchildren, and . . . tends his
rose . . . gardens with his beautiful . . .
young . . . wife.

DOLORES
His young wife . . . has . . . grandchildren?

TOM
Well. He . . . married again when his,
first wife was tragically . . . sucked out
the window of a . . . DC 10, could I get
another drink?

DOLORES
What?!

BARRELLER signals for another drink.

BARRELLER
Out of a plane?

TOM
Yes. A man of many private sorrows.
Each one . . . of . . . them . . . etched . . .
on that . . . gaunt . . . Sicilian . . . face.

BARRELLER
Is this where the rage comes from?

TOM
I think that's probably . . . quite a . . .
perceptive remark, Barreller. Their
autumn years denied them. Watching
the leaves turn golden without her. The
apples falling from the trees.

DOLORES
You mean the roses . . . ?

TOM

Well . . . there's obviously an orchard
too.

BARRELLER

It must be quite a place.

A drink arrives for TOM. Again he skulls it, his hand trembling a little.

. . . Eh . . . Cheers.

TOM just nods over the rim of the rapidly disappearing pint.

You see that's what I'd like too, Clive.
Security. That's why. That's why I'm
going completely legitimate. With an
office and a secretary and everything.
Something to pass on. Otherwise I'd go
ga ga. I suppose I'm like Mr Magniani,
in that regard. Family.

TOM

Family. In that regard.

DOLORES
(fondly)
I think that Guinness has hit you a little
bit has it Clive?

TOM

Not being Irish. I have no head for
strong drink.

BARRELLER

You're among friends, Clive. If you can't
cut loose once in a while, what way
would you end up?

TOM

Dublin. Last jewel of the empire! Fading
dowager among so many dowdy aunts!

DOLORES

Are you trying to say you like it?

TOM

Like a twin I never knew I had, Dolores.

DOLORES

Why don't you give us a song?

TOM

Whereas some people say business and
pleasure are inseparable, Mr Magnani

41

would have my guts for garters were he
to see how much I've already intruded
upon your hospitality. And besides, I
never sing. Never.

50.   INT. SAME A LITTLE LATER

TOM and DOLORES are singing a duet with the Karaoke machine.

> Although I know I've only met you
> Something tells me that I won't forget you
> It's like you're sent from heaven above
> It feels so right, it must be love
>
> I turned my back on sly romance
> Thought I'd led a merry dance
>
> Could this be love?

They are greeted with loud applause. They stand there for a moment.
DOLORES looking at TOM. TOM looking over his glasses at DOLORES.
It's then a little awkward. Suddenly, there's a flash of terror across
TOM'S face.

                    TOM
          Oh my God. What time is it?

                    DOLORES
          It's early. It's only ten past nine.

                    TOM
          The play!!

                    DOLORES
          The what?

                    TOM
          The . . . the plane. I have to catch my
          plane!

                    DOLORES
          Get a later one.

TOM despairs at her disappointment.

                    TOM
          I can't. I'm sorry. I can't,

He goes to BARRELLER.

                    TOM
          Barreller. I have to go.

                    BARRELLER
          Do you want a lift to the airport?

TOM

The airport? No. No thanks. I'm fine. I'll
get a cab. Bye. Goodbye Dolores.

DOLORES

Okay. See you.

TOM rushes towards the door.

DOLORES

Clive! Wait!

He turns. She is holding the suitcase towards him. He returns and
hesitantly, guiltily, he takes it.

TOM

Thanks.

DOLORES

Take care.

TOM

You too.

He looks at the suitcase. He doesn't want to leave. But he does. DOLORES
looks at the door when he is gone.

51.   EXT. STREET IN DUBLIN EVENING

TOM attempts to hail taxis. He can't get one. He is looking at his watch, he
starts to run.

52.   EXT. THEATRE NIGHT

TOM, still in costume as 'Cllve', runs to the stage door. He bangs on it.
The STAGE DOORMAN opens it and doesn't recognise him.

TOM
(cockney accent)
It's me! Tommy! (Dublin accent.) I mean
Tommy! I'm due on!

He tries to remove his moustache. It won't budge. He nearly pulls his head
off. He looks up imploringly at the DOORMAN who just shuts the door.

53.   EXT. THEATRE NIGHT

TOM runs around the front of the theatre and into the empty foyer.

54.   INT. FOYER NIGHT

TOM goes to the box office where the ATTENDANT is pulling down a
blind.

                              TOM
          Wait! Wait!

                           ATTENDANT
          Shh! There's a show on.

                              TOM
          I'm in it!

                           ATTENDANT
          I beg your pardon?

                              TOM
          I need a ticket. I've got to get in!

                           ATTENDANT
          We don't admit latecomers. I'm sorry.

     She pulls down the blind. TOM attempts to take the moustache off again.
     It's stuck fast.

                              TOM
          Please!

55.   EXT. THEATRE NIGHT

      TOM runs around the side of the theatre. He comes to a ladder riveted into
      the wall. He begins to climb it.

56.   EXT. ROOF OF THE THEATRE NIGHT

      TOM climbs onto the roof of the theatre and runs over to the fly tower.
      There's a door in it, he wrenches it open and goes in.

57.   INT. FLY TOWER NIGHT

      TOM steps on to a gantry very high above the stage. The production is in
      progress. It seems like miles down. TOM sees a laundry basket he opens
      it and looks through it frantically.

58.   INT. ONSTAGE NIGHT

      O'MALLEY and the rest of the cast are well into the play. Act IV sc iv.

                           O'MALLEY
          Where is the power then, to beat him back?
          Where be thy tenants and thy followers?
          Are they now upon the western shore?
          Safe conducting the rebels from their ships?

                           ACTOR 1
                          (as Derby)
          No, my good lord, My friends are in the north.

O'MALLEY
Cold friends to me. What do they in the north?
When they should serve their sovereign in the west?

59.   INT. THE WINGS NIGHT

THE STAGE MANAGER speaks into his headset.

STAGE MANAGER
He's still not here? Okay. We'll get
someone to do his lines.

60.   INT. FLY TOWER NIGHT

High above the stage on the gantry TOM has found a swastika flag in the
laundry basket. It'll have to do as a 'costume'. He wraps it around himself
and begins to check how secure various ropes are.

61.   INT. ONSTAGE NIGHT

Enter a MESSENGER.

ACTOR 2
(playing Messenger 1)
My gracious sovereign now in Devonshire,
As I by my friends are well advertised
Sir Edward Courtney and the haughty prelate,
Bishop of Exeter, his elder brother,
With many more confederates are in view.

62.   INT. FLYTOWER NIGHT

TOM grabs a rope and begins to slide down towards the stage saying his
to himself

TOM
(quietly)
'My lord, the army of great Buckingham . . .
My lord, the army of great Buckingham . . .
My lord the army of great Buckingham.'

63.   INT. ONSTAGE NIGHT

Enter another MESSENGER. In the wings we see the STAGE MANAGER
hand ACTOR I a wig and a hat. He is now MESSENGER 3 – Tom's part

ACTOR 3
(playing Messenger 2)
In Kent, my liege, the Guildfords are in arms;
And every hour more competitors
Flock to the rebels. and their power grows strong.

64.   INT. FLY TOWER NIGHT

TOM'S progress down towards the stage continues. Suddenly it gives way and he plummets.

65.   ONSTAGE NIGHT

Enter MESSENGER 3

> ACTOR 1
> (playing Messenger 3)
> My lord, the army of great Buckingham –

TOM lands on him. Knocking him to the floor in a heap. TOM recovers, sitting there in his dress and his moustache.

> TOM
> The news I have to tell your majesty
> Is that by sudden floods and fall of waters
> Buckingham's army dispers'd and scatter'd:
> And he himself wandered away alone,
> No man knows whither.

66.   INT. NIGHT

TOM is shaving off his false moustache. O'MALLEY sits playing with the money. He is hysterical.

> O'MALLEY
> I don't fucking believe it! I mean, I
> wouldn't, but if I wanted to, I could go
> right now and stay the night in Tubbets-
> town Castle. Ten grand a night. A castle
> all to myself.

TOM shoots him a look.

> O'MALLEY
> I wouldn't. That would be insane,
> obviously. But I could . . . if I were
> insane enough, I mean. You know, I
> knew you could do it. I always said you
> could do it. But I just didn't fucking
> believe it!

> TOM
> You see, Anthony, acting . . .

> O'MALLEY
> Yes?

> TOM
> . . . is a craft. It's not a trade.

46

O'MALLEY

What does that mean?

TOM

It means . . .

O'MALLEY

Yes . . .

TOM

. . . you have to live it,

O'MALLEY

You're beginning to gloat. I just knew
you were going to be unbearable.

TOM

I'm not gloating. I feel awful. They,
didn't strike me as dangerous criminals
in the least. They were very decent.

O'MALLEY

Believe me they're not. Barreller told me
some stories that'd make your skin
crawl.

TOM

Well . . . The real scary thing about it?

O'MALLEY

Yes?

TOM

Was me. I mean, I knew I wasn't Clive.
I knew I was me. But I was going to kiss
Dolores!

O'MALLEY

Oh. Really?

TOM

Oh yeah. I was complete. I was
confident. I was going to be someone
else and try to begin something with
her! Jesus! What was I doing?

O'MALLEY

You were acting.

TOM

(stops shaving for a moment)
I . . . suppose (hope) I was.

O'MALLEY
Now you know . . . (the pain).

TOM
Tell me about you and Dolores.

O'MALLEY
Me and Dolores?

TOM
You're going to get her 'trained', yeah?

O'MALLEY
Well. One does what one can. For the
younger . . .

TOM
Bollocks.

O'MALLEY
She's a little ride. What do you want me
to say?

TOM
I think she liked Clive.

O'MALLEY
Who's Clive?

TOM
My character.

O'MALLEY
(indignant)
Well she can never see him again.

TOM
What was the money for?

O'MALLEY
Stolen cars or something,

TOM
From Magnani?

O'MALLEY
I suppose so.

TOM finishes shaving. He is himself again. O'MALLEY pours them both a
glass of whiskey. They clink glasses.

O'MALLEY
To you . . .

TOM
Whoever that is . . .

They drink the whiskey.

> TOM
>
> Is he tough?

> O'MALLEY
>
> Who, Barreller or Magnani?

> TOM
>
> Well . . . both . . .

> O'MALLEY
>
> Oh stop worrying. We'll never need to
> know.

67.   INT. RITA'S HOUSE 8.30 AM

MARY, ready for school, opens the front door to a terrified looking
O'MALLEY. TOM stands behind her, putting his coat on.

> O'MALLEY
>
> Give me a drink of water!

68.   EXT. PARK MORNING

The leafy avenue on the way to school. TOM, O'MALLEY and MARY walk
along.

> O'MALLEY
>
> First of all, I don't know what possessed
> me. An actors curiosity I suppose. I
> slipped on down to the Baltic last night,
> just to see. Just to see how effective
> you'd been. And to see what Dolores . . .
> thought of you and . . . I don't know, it's
> all that bollocks about returning to the
> scene of the crime and everything.

> TOM
>
> What happened?

> O'MALLEY
>
> Well, Barrell . . .

He signals that he doesn't want to say any names in front of MARY.

> O'MALLEY
>
> Our certain party wasn't there. He was . . .

> MARY
>
> The certain party who owed the money
> to the other certain party. Neither party
> having ever met?

O'MALLEY stops in his tracks.

> TOM

> She knows.

> O'MALLEY

> She knows? What does she know?

MARY sits on a bench. Her hands in her pockets, legs swinging.

> MARY

> I know everything. And you should give
> me some of the money as well.

> TOM

> She helped me. With my character.

> O'MALLEY

> Who else fucking helped you?

> MARY

> Watch the language, meester.

> TOM

> No one. She kind of directed me.

> O'MALLEY

> Have you lost the head entirely?

> TOM

> I know. It's weird. I know. Just. Just tell
> us. What happened?

O'MALLEY looks at MARY. He gives in. He sits on the bench.

> O'MALLEY

> Barreller wasn't there. But Dolores was.
> And I don't know. I just knew by her,
> when you know her like I do, that
> something was amiss, you know?

> TOM

> They knew they'd been done?

> O'MALLEY

> She said that someone had rang from
> Magnani. Someone real. To arrange
> about getting the money.

> TOM

> And the shit hit the fan.

> O'MALLEY

> Well, obviously. Barreller insisted he'd
> just given their man, Clive, the full
> payment. The Magnani people threw a

freaker. Tom. They're sending someone
over.

TOM

Poor Barreller.

O'MALLEY

Fuck Barreller, what about me?

MARY

('Mind the language')

Hey.

O'MALLEY

Oh fuck off.

TOM

What do you mean what about you?

O'MALLEY

Well, Dolores starts on at me about did
Dad ever tell me about the deal? He has
a loose tongue sometimes. He likes
talking to me and so on . . .

TOM

And did you blab to anyone about it . . .

O'MALLEY

. . . Because no one else could have
known. And this person they're sending
over. He'll probably want to talk, to me!!
I mean I didn't let on I knew anything
about it. I was brilliant, I think she
bought it. But Jesus. This could be a
fucking hitman!! They might torture me
or anything!

MARY

Calm down. You're acting like a baby.

O'MALLEY

Sometimes you're entitled, okay? This is
heavy. I can hardly breathe. Okay?

He is on the verge of tears.

MARY

Relax the cacks. When is this hitman
coming?

O'MALLEY

Today! He's flying in at twelve. And
going straight to the Baltic bar.

MARY looks at TOM.

> MARY
>
> There's only one thing for it.

69.   INT. AIRPORT ARRIVALS DAY

Among those waiting for loved ones or business clients is a man holding
two signs. 'Are you from Magnani?' 'I'm Barreller!' He wears a shell suit,
sunglasses and a baseball cap. It's TOM. He has a big pot belly and a
blond wig. He chews gum furiously. He nervously watches every person
emerging from baggage collection. A HUGE MANIAC with scars all over
his face comes out and stands looking around for a moment.

> TOM
>
> Good fuck . . .

A pretty YOUNG WOMAN runs into the HUGE MANIAC'S arms. TOM
breathes a sigh of relief. Then there's an immaculately dressed short guy
standing in front of TOM. He's like a jockey. He has a neat little moustache.
He speaks in a very broad Scottish accent. He munches popcorn furiously.

> JOCK
>
> Barreller?

> TOM
>
> That's the name. The name of me. Are
> you from Magnani?

> JOCK
>
> I wasnae expecting to be picked up.

> TOM
>
> Well. It's the least I could do. Given the
> unfortunate . . . circumstances. (As if
> this will solve the situation.) And I'm
> going to buy you some lunch.

> JOCK
>
> Fucking right it's the least you could do!

> TOM
>
> ('Typical! I have to put up with this')
> Ah don't start. I'm not in the mood,
> alright!

They start to walk.

> JOCK
>
> I don't care what fucking mood you're
> in! You've got a lot of explaining to do!

> TOM
>
> Ah fuck up! Don't, alright? Just don't!

Are you all right? Here, what's wrong
with your eyes?

                    JOCK
          It's stress-related. It's all right. I just
          need you to apply some pressure
          between my shoulder blades.

TOM embraces JOCK.

                    TOM
          Like this?

                    JOCK
          Yes, a little higher.

We hear a clicking noise.

                    JOCK
          That's it

                    TOM
          You're okay now?

                    JOCK
          Ya, it's just, it's very embarrassing.

They walk off.

70.   INT. RESTAURANT DAY

TOM and JOCK sit in an Italian restaurant in by the sea. Nearby
O'MALLEY and MARY sit eating lunch also, observing. O'MALLEY wears
a baseball cap with Far & Away on it. They eat big plates of messy pasta
with sauce. TOM eats as though he is very hungry. TOM'S performance is
110 per cent commitment. He's absolutely bonkers. O'MALLEY and MARY
are deeply impressed.

                    JOCK
          I'm no' gonnae airbrush the situation
          here, Barreller. The lads over in London
          have gone fucking bananas about this.
          I've never seen them this bad. They
          want this fucker killed.

                    TOM
          Well I do as well and Magnani's upset.
          okay, but let's not spend our lives rolling
          around in the past and who's responsible
          for what. It becomes tedious.

                    JOCK
          Well, the world would be a nicer place if
          we all took your advice, I'm sure. But

53

Magnani's having a caniption. I've never
seen her like this.

                    TOM
You've never seen her, like this? What
the fuck are you talking about?

                    JOCK
I mean I've never ever seen her want a
man tortured as bad as this.

                    TOM
No just. I didn't know he was a woman.

                    JOCK
A lot of people make that mistake. It's a
sexist thing. It's like just because you're
a woman, you're not allowed to have a
ruthless reputation. It's quite sad when
you think about it. Don't stereotype her,
Barreller. It's a dangerous mistake.

                    TOM
Sometimes I feel like a big mist comes
down me. I'm very much a man of my
fists, Jock.

                    JOCK
Any . . . way. Who ripped us off?

                    TOM
I don't know. An English bloke. Nice
chap. Clive.

                    JOCK
Clive.

                    TOM
That's it. That's all I know.

                    JOCK
Would you recognise him again?

                    TOM
(as though he has a great talent for faces)
I think I would, you know? Very,
handsome looking fella. Big glasses on
him. I just assumed he was your man.

                    JOCK
You just assumed? Just because
someone tells you that they're someone
you just assume that's who they are.
I must say I find that idiotic, Barreller.

                    TOM
Hey, hey, easy on the casual insults
flying around there, Jock. It could
happen to anyone. I'm buying you lunch
here and everything. Don't start the
mean Scottish bollocks. It makes me
feel tired.

                    JOCK
Here, now you take it easy. It's one thing
me calling you an imbecile because you
gave our money to some bloke just
because he had glasses or something.
But you're getting into a whole racist
area which is quite fucked up, frankly,
alright?

                    TOM
Oh, you're great on the old 'that's sexist,
and that's racist' What are you the
fucking . . . army, or someone? Nobody
tells me what to do!

                    JOCK
You've obviously failed to grasp what's
happening here. Most people in your
position would tend to be slightly a bit
more contrite. What are you attacking
me for?

                    TOM
'Cause it was obviously someone from
your side. ripped us off!

                    JOCK
What!!

A WAITER approaches.

                    WAITER
Is everything alright, sir?

                    TOM
Fuck off. This is a business lunch here,
alright?

                    WAITER
I'm sorry. Excuse me.

                    JOCK
You're attracting attention to us and
everything.

Fuck them! Fuck them all! The bastards!

JOCK'S eyes cross. TOM gets up wordlessly and embraces JOCK. We hear
a clicking noise. TOM sits back down. JOCK lets the startled restaurant
settle. And waits for 'Barreller' to calm down a little. O'MALLEY is shitting
himself. MARY beams unphased pride and amusement.

JOCK

Where do you get it that it was someone
from our side that did it?

TOM

'Cause no one here knew anything
about it.

JOCK

What about this . . . actor you were . . .
helping? What the fuck was that about?

O'MALLEY goes pale.

TOM

He wouldn't know anything. All he knew
was I owed money to someone. We all
owe money to someone. Anyway he's a
moron. And the fucker can't act.

O'MALLEY spits his drink out all over MARY. She patiently wipes her face
with her napkin.

JOCK

He knew nothing about Magnani?

TOM

Nothing.

JOCK

You're sure?

TOM

Ask me that one more time and you can
pay for your own lunch.

JOCK

I don't mind paying for my own lunch,
Barreller. That's the least of my concerns.
I'm trying to get to the bottom of this
fiasco. I'll pay for my own fucking lunch!

TOM

I'm paying for it! And it's not a fiasco,
right? Here.

TOM puts a suitcase on the table.

                    JOCK
        What's this?

                    TOM
        It's Clive's. He forgot it when he fucked
        off.

                    JOCK
        What's in it?

                    TOM
        Clues, Jock. Clues.

                    JOCK
        What clues?

                    TOM
        I don't know. It's locked.

                    JOCK
        So how do you know it's got clues in it?

                    TOM
                (exasperated)
        I presume it has! Jesus . . .

                    JOCK
        For fuck's sake . . .

He takes his knife and begins to pick the lock. The WAITERS and other
DINERS are all equally interested at this stage. TOM continues to eat his
lunch. JOCK clicks the briefcase and opens it. He begins to take out the
contents. JOCK takes out an envelope. In the envelope are plane tickets.

                    JOCK
        Tickets from Heathrow to Dublin.

                    TOM
        What did I say? What did I say?

                    JOCK
        Alright. Don't have a . . . party.

JOCK takes out a brochure for the Aran Islands.

                    JOCK
        Where's the . . . Aran Islands?

                    TOM
        In the west. Good place to hide out.
        A very good place.

                    JOCK
        Do you think we should go there?

                          TOM
                       (laughing)
            I'm not going! It's your money!

                          JOCK
            I don't believe this.

JOCK'S eyes cross.

                          JOCK
            You lost it. And you can recognise him.

TOM gets up again and embraces JOCK. We hear a clicking noise.
TOM sits back down

                          TOM
            Ah . . . he's English, you'll find him. It's
            not a big place.

                          JOCK
                      (bewilderment)
            You're a fucking headcase. When I tell
            Magnani about the lack of cooperation
            you've shown. She'll go mental.

                          TOM
            Ah eat your dinner.

                          JOCK
            . . . Incredible . . .

                          TOM
            Is it good, yeah? I'm getting it, okay? I'm
            getting it. It's the least I can do.

JOCK just shakes his head.

                          TOM
                     (calling Waiter)
            Hey, Padre. Lebillerooney.
            Mawshaydohollay.

71.   EXT. HOWTH HARBOUR DAY

TOM as 'Barreller' is seeing JOCK onto a fishing trawler in Howth harbour.

                          JOCK
            How tall is this Clive fella?

                          TOM
            Ah, about my height.

JOCK considers the boat. The SKIPPER stands there counting a bundle of
money.

JOCK

And this is the only way to get there?

TOM

The only way way to get to an 'island' is
across the 'sea.'

JOCK
(climbing down into the trawler)
If I don't find him, I'm coming straight
back. You still owe Magnani fifty
thousand.

TOM

Yeah, yeah. Stop . . . moaning!

JOCK

Moaning . . . !

TOM

It's an annoying and fatiguing
characteristic!

JOCK

Coming from someone as balanced as
you, pal, I'll have to take that on board.

TOM

Good man.

The SKIPPER prepares to cast away. TOM walks away turning to wave at
the SKIPPER, who waves back. JOCK stands on the deck, uncomfortable
and uncertain.

72.   EXT. HOWTH HARBOUR DAY

TOM. looks up at O'MALLEY and MARY who are at the window of the
restaurant. They are applauding.

73.   INT. BATHROOM IN RITA'S HOUSE DAY

TOM is removing his disguise, washing himself, removing false eyebrows,
etc. He is quoting from Richard Ill. Act V sc iii.

TOM

What do I fear? Myself? There's none else by;
Richard loves Richard, that is I and I.
Is there a murderer here? No. Yes, I am!
Then fly. What, from myself

He resembles himself again. He says to the mirror . . .

TOM

My conscience hath a thousand several tongues,

And every tongue brings in a several tale,
And every tale condemns me for a villain.

74. INT. THEATRE DAY

The Richard III set is still being struck by the STAGE HANDS. There is a
lot less of it left now and the theatre looks more desolate and temporary.

> MARY
> Why do grown-up people become
> frightened? They're frightened because
> they don't know what's going to happen.
> They imagine the worst, They think the
> worst is going to happen. But they can't
> even imagine the worst. Like
> Shakespeare says, 'The worst is not, so
> long as we can say. 'This is the worst.'
>
> For people to calm down, I've found that
> you need to love them. And the way to
> love them is to remember that everyone
> is just a little kid. They're all just
> frightened little kids imagining the
> worst.

We see MARY holding O'MALLEY'S hand in the park. where they were for
Sc. 68. But O'MALLEY is just a tiny BOY, lost in O'MALLEY's clothes. He
stares up at her fearfully.

> MARY
> They need to hold your hand.
> Remember that and you can even
> forgive anyone who betrayed you. They
> did it because they were frightened and
> alone and they needed to hold
> someone's hand. There's a few people
> in this story who need a lot of
> hand-holding. Just like in the world.
> There are some betrayers too.

75. EXT. THE PARK DAY

TOM and O'MALLEY walk towards a bandstand. They carry takeout cups
of coffee for themselves and an ice cream for MARY.

> O'MALLEY
> Are you alright?
>
> TOM
> I just feel weird.

O'MALLEY

I don't doubt it.

TOM

But that was mad weird. I was actually
having . . . memories.

O'MALLEY

You became Barreller.

TOM

No, made up memories. Of a made up
Barreller. A sort of very, thick and violent
Barreller.

O'MALLEY

No doubt an aspect of yourself.

TOM

That I'm thick and violent?

O'MALLEY

That you have an aspect.

TOM

You're saying that I have an aspect to
myself that's both thick and violent?

O'MALLEY

In order to be convincing.

TOM

You're saying that if you were to
describe me to someone, you'd say,
'Well there's a decent side to Tom, but
there's also an aspect to him that's very
thick and violent'?

O'MALLEY

You're over-reacting to what is at root a
compliment.

TOM

You're praising my ignorant and violent
nature.

O'MALLEY

That you found it.

TOM

You're full of shit.

O'MALLEY

Within yourself.

                    TOM
Perhaps you've overlooked something.

                    O'MALLEY
I'm open to debate.

                    TOM
That maybe I can act?

                    O'MALLEY
No maybe about it.

                    TOM
Thank you.

                    O'MALLEY
But to be so convincing.

                    TOM
Yes.

                    O'MALLEY
Think about it.

                    TOM
It's about judgement.

                    O'MALLEY
As Richard for instance. I find within
myself the dark places.

                    TOM
Perhaps you don't have to look too deep.

                    O'MALLEY
And I won't deny that.

                    TOM
Thank you.

                    O'MALLEY
I never said I was moral.

                    TOM
I know.

                    O'MALLEY
Just admit one thing.

                    TOM
Yes?

                    O'MALLEY
That I was right.

                    TOM
That you were right.

O'MALLEY
You are learning. From this.

TOM
That's true. I'm fucking learning alright.

They reach the bandstand. MARY sits on the floor colouring an elaborate chart which displays their situation in a graphic form. Each of the main players assigned a colour and so on. A DOG mooches around the bandstand as though keeping her company or protecting her.

O'MALLEY
And we are sad men. Standing here
awaiting the advice of a nine-year-old
girl.

TOM
However. We are big enough to accept it.

O'MALLEY
And from that we take faint comfort.

TOM
It's all we ever get.

O'MALLEY
And now we desist before we wallow in
self-pity.

TOM
Good.

O'MALLEY
Nice talk.

MARY
If a little pompous. We have to kill Clive.

She presents the chart. For such an intelligent young girl it still looks like the work of a child. TOM and O'MALLEY shudder.

MARY
You see. This Aran Islands plan is only
of any use in the short term.

TOM
He'll come back.

MARY
It was an emergency. What the hell.

O'MALLEY
He's going to come back. And he'll still
want his money.

                        MARY

Exactly. So the medium term solution is
to kill Clive, the character. And present
Magnani with the problem that the
money may be irrevocably lost along
with Clive. And hope they give up.

                        TOM

What if Magnani still holds Barreller
responsible? Clive's dead, the money's
gone. It's still Barreller's fault.

                        MARY

That's the long-term plan here. The
beauty is that Barreller and Magnani
have never met. And they must never
meet.

O'MALLEY looks anxious.

                        MARY

Because once Magnani knows who you
are, things could turn unpleasant.

                        O'MALLEY

Which I would like to avoid, if at all
possible.

                        MARY

Well, that's the idea. And only a moron
would need to state it.

                        TOM

What were we thinking?

                        O'MALLEY

I continually . . . cut you slack young
lady. And I'm not beyond having you
disciplined. (Indicating part of the
chart.) What's this plan?

                        MARY

That's the Super Longest Term
Copperfasten Plan.

                        O'MALLEY

Which is?

                        MARY

To invent a time machine, go back in
time and never have to put this whole
scheme into operation.

                    O'MALLEY
And the chances of that would be . . .

                    MARY
To put it scientifically, 'not brilliant'. But
the first thing we can try is killing Clive
off.

                    TOM
Kill my character.

                    MARY
Yes.

                    TOM
Who'll kill him?

                    MARY
You will.

                    TOM
What? How?

                    MARY
You have to present yourself to Barreller
again.

                    TOM
As Clive?

                    MARY
No.

                    TOM
As myself?

                    MARY
No.

                    TOM
As who, then?

76.   INT. COCK AND WEATHERVANE DAY

BARRELLER and DOLORES sit opposite TOM who wears a red wig, buck
teeth and huge padding in his cheeks. RONNIE and LESLEY also sit there.
No one says anything. TOM eats a mountain of popcorn furiously.

                    BARRELLER
Can I . . . get you anything, Jock?

                    TOM
              (excellent Scottish accent)
I'm probably gonnae need more
popcorn, Barreller.

                       65

BARRELLER

O . . . kay. We can get that for you.

BARRELLER looks to LESLEY who goes to get some.

TOM

I need to keep eating popcorn. It helps
me convince myself that I'm at the
pictures. That way I can just about live
with the intense brutality I'm required to
inflict on people. As if it's not real, you
know?

BARRELLER

Okay. I'm very much out of my depth
here, you know?

TOM

Well just do your best, alright?

BARRELLER

We thought you were coming yesterday.

TOM

The plane was . . . a day late.

BARRELLER

. . . Right . . .

LESLEY gives TOM the popcorn. TOM acknowledges him.

TOM

I don't say thanks, big man, okay? It's
just something I don't do.

LESLEY

Okay.

TOM

Don't want to lose my edge.

BARRELLER

. . . Okay . . .

TOM

Alright. Who knew about your deal with
Mr Magnani?

BARRELLER

Just us. Me. My daughter. And my sons,
Ronnie and Lesley. And even . . .
Ronnie's not all there, or anything, you
know? (Addressing Ronnie.) You
probably don't know who Mr Magnani
is, Ronnie, do you?

                    RONNIE
                    (thinks)
No.

                    BARRELLER
And Lesley's deaf in one ear.

                    TOM
No one else.

BARRELLER looks at DOLORES.

                    TOM
What's that? What's that look about?

                    BARRELLER
It's impossible. But I was helping this . . .
actor . . . with some . . . stories.

                    DOLORES
He's . . . he's an actor and he was
researching . . . villains . . .

                    BARRELLER
This place is usually full of lowlifes.

                    DOLORES
He thought that Dad was more of a
serious criminal than . . . he is . . .

                    TOM
Well, how serious are you?

                    BARRELLER
Ah Jaysus. I've handled a few stolen
cars, in my time, like. Just like the five
Jags we got from Mr Magnani. Over on
the ferry. Easy to get rid of. But I'm
going completely legitimate. I've bought
a share in this place. And I'm – (Clears
throat.) – getting an office with a . . .
secretary. But I . . . probably talked
myself up to a little bit more than that,
you know?

                    TOM
To this actor.

                    BARRELLER
Yes.

TOM begins eating the popcorn furiously.

                        BARRELLER
I was helping him! It was harmless!
A bit of crack!

                        TOM

Crack?

                        BARRELLER
                    (smiling hopefully)
A bit of a laugh! (No smile.) Fun.

                        TOM
Fun . . . What, specifically, did you tell
him about Mr Magnani?

                        BARRELLER
Nothing. Just that in the shady world
of outside the normal procedures of
everyday life. That was possible for a
certain party to . . . owe money to
another certain party, neither party
having ever . . . met.

                        TOM
And did you happen to casually,
fucking, mention that you might be such
a certain party, in a similar . . . scheme
of things?

                        BARRELLER

Yes.

                        TOM
And he could have easily given this
information to someone. Someone,
perhaps of . . . acting abilities that
border on genius. Someone who could
come and fool you?

                        BARRELLER
Maybe. I don't know. I'm just really,
sorry. I wish I could pay you. I really do.

                        TOM
Ah ah, don't torture yourself. I never
allow people to torture . . . themselves.

TOM allows some menace to engulf them.

                        TOM
So this fellow who took the money

                        BARRELLER
Clive.

                            68

TOM

Clive. Clive what?

BARRELLER

Just Clive was all he said.

TOM

From a female perspective, Dolores, was
he good looking, charming, perhaps
even a little sexually attractive?

DOLORES

Em . . .

BARRELLER

Ah, here . . .

TOM

I'm trying to get a picture!

DOLORES

He was . . . nice . . .

TOM

Nice . . .

BARRELLER

Spoke about Mr Magnani having roses
and how his wife was sucked out the
window of a DC10.

TOM

Mm. That actually happened to her
twice.

BARRELLER

What!!

TOM

Ah, it was a freak fucking thing. Well this
is obviously someone whose done their
research. Or it could be someone . . .
who knows him. Bears him a grudge.
Which narrows it down . . .

BARRELLER

Yeah?

TOM

To about a million fucking people!
I better talk to this actor see who he's
been blabbing to.

DOLORES

Em, maybe . . .

                              TOM
         Yes?

                            DOLORES
         Maybe I should talk to him.

                              TOM
         (I'm) not with you, doll.

                            DOLORES
         He's harmless . . . he's . . .

                           BARRELLER
         He's a poof. His name is O'Malley.

                            DOLORES
         Just. I'm not saying you're scary or
         anything, but if he did . . . become,
         scared, and went to the police.

                              TOM
         You want the gentle approach.

                            DOLORES
         He mightn't have told anyone
         intentionally.

                              TOM
         Alright. Maybe you have a point.
         Besides, Sometimes a beautiful young
         woman can be just as persuasive as a
         mindless act of terrifying physical
         assault. Don't you find?

                            DOLORES
         I'd . . . think so.

                              TOM
         However, if you don't get results, the key
         words in tomorrow's newspaper will be
         Actor, Merciless, Kidney and, quite
         possibly, Big Spoon.

Some of the padding in TOM'S mouth falls out. One of his cheeks
collapses. The others look at him, a bit aghast.

                              TOM
         All the salt in this popcorn. It's
         beginning to rot my face

77.   INT. THEATRE NIGHT

O'MALLEY and CAST are onstage. He speaks some lines from Act IV sc iv.
TOM watches him. A group of LEAVING CERT SCHOOLGIRLS are in the

                              70

audience in uniforms with their TEACHER. They hold playscripts of
Richard III. They are rapt by O'MALLEY'S performance.

> O'MALLEY
> Look what is done cannot be now amended.
> Men shall deal unadvisedly sometimes,
> Which after-hours gives leisure to repent.
> If I did take the kingdom from your sons,
> To make amends I'll give it to your daughter.
> If I have kill'd the issue of your womb,
> To quicken your increase I will beget
> Mine issue of your blood upon your daughter.

78.   INT. THEATRE NIGHT

Another dismal curtain call. TOM is absolutely wrecked. He stands bowing
beleaguerdly beside a magnanimous O'MALLEY, who bows especially for
the UNIFORMED SCHOOLGIRLS,

> TOM
> Can we please just give the money
> back?

> O'MALLEY
> After everything we've been through?

> TOM
> I don't care.

> O'MALLEY
> Well, you might be a selfish little cur.
> But at this point, the money's my only
> comfort.

> TOM
> What the fuck are you talking about?
> The lion's share has to be mine. I've
> worked my hole off.

The audience are leaving. ACTORS leave the curtain call. O'MALLEY bows
to the very, last forlorn clap.

> TOM
> Oh God. How is it I'm so good at fooling
> people in real life and as soon as I set
> foot in the theatre I'm shit?

> O'MALLEY
> Barreller's not expecting to meet an
> actor. These people are.

TOM looks at the audience filing out. The curtain comes down.

79.   INT. BACKSTAGE NIGHT

TOM and O'MALLEY come backstage and drink some coffee in the wings.

>   TOM
>   What's worse is, I like Barreller. And
>   Dolores. And we're putting them
>   through agony.

>   O'MALLEY
>   'I will converse with iron witted fools.'

>   TOM
>   We shouldn't be stealing from him. It's
>   wrong. He's not even a real crook.

>   O'MALLEY
>   We're not stealing from him. We're
>   robbing Magnani.

>   TOM
>   Who could be the biggest headcase m
>   Europe, you know?

O'MALLEY produces one of MARY'S elaborate charts on a piece of A4 paper.

>   O'MALLEY
>   Just stick to Mary's plan. I tell Dolores
>   how to contact 'Clive'. You be Clive. We
>   fake Clive's death. Dolores tells
>   Barreller.

DOLORES has come in the stage door and is talking to the DOORMAN who points down the corridor towards the dressing rooms.

>   O'MALLEY
>   Barreller tells Magnani we found Clive,
>   he spent your money but he's dead.
>   No, wait, no, yes, yes, Clive's dead
>   so Magnani can do what he she or it
>   fucking likes. Because the culprit's dead!
>   And we spend the dosh. It's that . . .
>   simple, don't back out now. We're so
>   close.

>   TOM
>   Oh shit.

>   O'MALLEY
>   What.

>   TOM
>   You're on.

                    O'MALLEY
        I haven't rehearsed! Who's Clive
        supposed to be?!

                    TOM
        I don't know! I can't be here. Improvise.

                    O'MALLEY
        I never improvise!

O'MALLEY wheels around, a big grin on his face.

                    O'MALLEY
        Dolores! What a pleasant surprise,

TOM dives into a dressing room to escape meeting DOLORES.

80.   INT. LADIES' DRESSING ROOM NIGHT

The dressing room is full of ACTRESSES in various states of undress. They
shout at TOM and throw things at him.

                    TOM
        Sorry! Sorry!

He backs out the door . . .

81.   INT. BACKSTAGE NIGHT

. . . And now draped in bras and lacy underwear, he comes face to face
with DOLORES. A chorus of ACTRESSES still shouting abuse at him.

                    O'MALLEY
        Em. Yes. Allow me to introduce a
        colleague. The inimitable Thomas
        Quirk.

                    DOLORES
                (looking at him strangely)
        . . . Hello . . .

                    TOM
                (with sickening terror)
        How's it . . . going?

                    DOLORES
        I've met you.

                    O'MALLEY
        The actor's curse! We have two lines in
        Braveheart, one of which is cut out, and
        we're recognisable forever!

                    DOLORES
        No. I've met you in person.

73

                              TOM
              I think I'd remember you. I have to go
              and wash these, em, bras for the
              actresses. So I'll . . .

                            DOLORES
              Okay. (She laughs.) It's weird, sorry.

O'MALLEY leads her away, looking over his shoulder at TOM.

                            O'MALLEY
              And what can I do for you, my love?
              How are the acting classes?

82.   INT. THEATRE NIGHT

TOM stands on stage peeping out from behind the curtains at . . .

83.   INT. THEATRE NIGHT

O'MALLEY and DOLORES who sit in the deserted stalls. This is
O'MALLEY'S shot at real-life acting. He makes a bollocks of it. Everything
he says seems both overblown and hollow at the same time.

                            DOLORES
              Dad is having some trouble Mr
              O'Malley.

                            O'MALLEY
              Oh . . . really? I'm sorry to hear that.

                            DOLORES
              Some people played a trick on us and
              they took some money.

                            O'MALLEY
              Oh no . . .

                            DOLORES
              And the money was for a man in
              England and he's very . . .

                            O'MALLEY
                        (a little too quickly)
              Well, understandably.

                            DOLORES
              Yeah . . . well. I know we've spoken
              about this before. you say you don't
              remember anything, but the thing is, is
              that Dad thinks he might have told you
              something about this money and you
              might have said something to
              somebody.

O'MALLEY
(racking his tiny brain)
Some money . . . some money . . . some
money . . . something about some money.
He may have. I don't know . . . Let me . . .

DOLORES
With someone in England.

O'MALLEY
Oh . . . The Certain Party . . .

DOLORES
Yes, that Dad owed money to.

O'MALLEY
(as though remembering how he once solved a pleasant puzzle)
A certain party owed money by another
certain party. Neither party having ever
met . . .

DOLORES
Yes.

O'MALLEY
Wonderful . . . yes . . .

DOLORES
Well I have to ask you if maybe you
might have said something, about that,
to someone.

O'MALLEY
Well. I'd like to think I'd have more tact,
Dolores. I mean . . . a position of trust is
not something I'd take lightly.

DOLORES
No one is accusing you. Mr O'Malley.
I'm just asking you to think about if you
might have mentioned it, in passing or
by, mistake. maybe. I'd be really,
grateful if you could help me.

O'MALLEY
(clearing his throat)
Your . . . gratitude is something I'd . . .
value. Highly.

DOLORES
You never said anything about it. To
anyone.

O'MALLEY

No. No.

And then a different kind of 'No' as he 'remembers' something very hammily. Day is dawning after months of night –

O'MALLEY

No . . . No!

DOLORES

Yes?

O'MALLEY

. . . Clive.

DOLORES

Yes! Clive! Tell me.

O'MALLEY

No . . . He wouldn't . . .

O'MALLEY is really going for it. He hangs onto the backs of seats. He looks like he's floating as his 'anguish' 'consumes' him. TOM, peeping out from behind the curtains, is wincing at the excess.

DOLORES

Who is he?

O'MALLEY

No . . .

DOLORES

I can help him. He could get hurt,

O'MALLEY

What would they do to him?

DOLORES

(commiserating)
I'm not sure. But we could help him.

O'MALLEY

He's my . . . cousin, Dolores. Moved here
a little while ago. Down on his luck, you
understand. And we were discussing
things. I . . . mentioned that I was
researching villains. I might have, I must
have . . . in passing, you understand.
Oh I'm so sorry.

DOLORES

Mr O'Malley. If you can tell me where he
is. If I can talk to him . . .

O'MALLEY

But I can't believe he'd . . .

76

                    DOLORES
          We might be able to help him.

                    O'MALLEY
          You can help him . . .

                    DOLORES
          I only met him briefly, but . . .

O'MALLEY'S ears prick up, as do TOM'S. She seems far away, thinking.
What does she think of CLIVE/TOM? O'MALLEY is becoming jealous.

                    O'MALLEY
          . . . yes?

                    DOLORES
          I don't think he'd . . .

                    O'MALLEY
          Yes?

                    DOLORES
          I mean I think there's . . .

                    O'MALLEY
          Yes

                    DOLORES
          I feel that he'd . . .

                    O'MALLEY
          Yes

                    DOLORES
          . . . listen to me.

                    O'MALLEY
          You want to help him? After everything
          he's done?

He takes her hand, looking down at it.,

                    O'MALLEY
          To . . . both of us?

                    DOLORES
          If I can get the money back. I might be
          able to stop them from hurting him.

                    O'MALLEY
          You don't feel that he deserves some
          violence? Some violence?

TOM looks on with amazement.

                         77

                    TOM
                 (to himself)
          What the fuck are you saying? You
          stupid twonk . . .

                   DOLORES
          I don't want to see anyone getting hurt.
          Where can I find him?

O'MALLEY looks at the curtain and then back at DOLORES, he's still
holding her hand.

                   O'MALLEY
          I see. Well if you feel that strongly about
          it, about him . . .

                   DOLORES
          I do.

                   O'MALLEY
          This is beginning to make sense. He
          said he needed to get away for a while.
          He owed some money and he needed to
          lie low.

                   DOLORES
          Where is he?

                   O'MALLEY
          He's . . . in . . .

                   DOLORES
          Yes . . .

                   O'MALLEY
          Tubbets . . . town Castle.

84.   EXT. STREET IN TEMPLE BAR NIGHT

TOM and O'MALLEY come down the street. O'MALLEY determined and
childish, hiding in his overcoat, TOM berating him.

                    TOM
          You stupid bollocks! You know how
          much that place costs? You don't think
          this is hard enough?

                   O'MALLEY
          You told me to improvise. I told you I
          can't improvise.

                    TOM
          Yeah, I told you to improvise. I didn't tell
          you to go completely off the fucking biff!

                    O'MALLEY
          Tom. Tom. Tubbetstown Castle . . .

                    TOM
          Yes?

They stop in the street.

                    O'MALLEY
          Felt right.

                    TOM
          You're an awful fucking eejit. Do you
          know that?

The UNIFORMED SCHOOLGIRLS approach O'MALLEY for his autograph.
He immediately turns on the charm. TOM begins to walk off.

                    O'MALLEY
          (to SCHOOLGIRLS, signing autographs)
          Did you enjoy the show? What are you
          girls doing in school uniforms? Surely
          you're too old for school. (To one
          especially.) Well you definitely are.

                    TOM
          (shouts)
          This is crazy! This is just so you can stay
          there for a night. Isn't it? Isn't it?

                    O'MALLEY
          Ignore him. ladies. (He taps he temple.)
          He has syphilis.

84a. EXT. TUBBETSTOWN CASTLE DAY

    A beautiful castle on an island.

84b. GRAND HALLWAY OF TUBBETSTOWN DAY

    MARY ushers the STAFF out.

                    MARY
          No, no that's fine we don't need
          anything else. Please leave. Please
          leave. That's right. We need nothing
          more than your magnificent
          surroundings. Get out. 'Til tomorrow
          then. Bye bye.

85.   INT. GRAND BALLROOM DAY

A squib filled with blood explodes on a tailor's dummy. O'MALLEY
clutches the detonator proudly. TOM is dressing as CLIVE. O'MALLEY
attaches explosive squibs to TOM'S chest, concealing them beneath his
shirt. Little bags of blood. Sunlight streams in the windows. O'MALLEY
places an earpiece receiver in his car.

                    O'MALLEY
       Okay the cue is, 'My balls swole up like
       a couple of grapefruit'. I'll blow the
       squibs. You're dead. Okay? 'My balls
       swole up like a couple of grapefruit.'
       I blow them.

TOM taps a tiny radio mic and barks loudly into it.

                    TOM
       Is this working?

Feedback squeals in O'MALLEY'S earpiece, he screams and rips it out.

                    O'MALLEY
       What are you trying to fucking do?!

                    TOM
       I need to know you can hear me! Here,
       wait, How am I suddenly going to start
       talking about my balls?

                    O'MALLEY
       You're an actor you'll work it into the
       fabric. Of the scene. I know you will.

                    TOM
       'Into the fabric.' I'll work my balls into
       the fabric.

MARY comes in and presses a remote control. Music starts playing. A
mirrorball starts spinning. TOM and MARY stand transfixed. O'MALLEY
grabs the remote and switches it all off.

                    O'MALLEY
       Tom . . . Focus. Now be ready. I was
       covered in these things in Excalibur.
       They hurt like fuck when they go off.

                    TOM
       You say that and I can almost hear the
       pleasure in your voice do you know
       that?

                    O'MALLEY
       One should suffer for their art.

TOM
Here, were there guns in Excalibur?

86.   EXT. BEACH ACROSS FROM TUBBETSTOWN ISLAND DAY

TOM as CLIVE gets a massive slap in the face from DOLORES. He is sent
sprawling. His glasses fly off. TOM quickly retrieves them from the sand
and feels the sting on his face. He goes towards a rowboat on the shore.

TOM
(holding boat)
You were absolutely entitled to do that.
What I did was wrong.

DOLORES
(climbing into boat)
I just couldn't believe it.

TOM
(pushing off)
I know.

DOLORES
You seemed so nice.

TOM
(rowing)
Don't. I know. I was vain. I wanted to see
if I could do it.

DOLORES
Well, now you know. Where are we
going?

TOM
To the money. I've hidden it where I'm
staying. I'm minding . . . a castle for
some . . . lords. Some . . . earls. The
Duke of Rich . . . ard.

87.   EXT. TUBBETSTOWN CASTLE ISLAND DAY

DOLORES and TOM arrive at the island, get out of the boat and go up
towards the castle.

DOLORES
What are you doing here?

TOM
Living, after a fashion. Hiding. From my
creditors. I've always looked for the easy
way out you see. The short cut. I don't
know what it is.

81

                    DOLORES
Look. I know. My dad was the same. But
people can change Clive. You just need
to make the effort.

                    TOM
I know I just need someone who can
show me. (Forlornly.) I'd never get
myself into these scrapes.

                    DOLORES
Can I ask you something? Why are you
so angry with me?

                    TOM
I'm a slave to my emotions. I don't know
why I expected you to understand.

                    DOLORES
Mr O'Malley said you were having some
bad luck. But I don't see how that's my
fault.

                    TOM
No. Not all bad. I met you. And you
know, maybe if I hadn't met you I still
wouldn't care.

                    DOLORES
                (softens slightly)
What are you saying?

                    TOM
I think I'm saying I wish I'd never gone
through with this.

They reach the castle.

87a.   INT. CASTLE DAY

TOM brings DOLORES into the castle.

                    TOM
This is the . . . castle.

                    DOLORES
                (genuine but muted)
Wow . . .

87b   INT. CASTLE DAY

TOM and DOLORES walk through the castle, both downcast.

                    DOLORES
          Listen, was it just me?

                    TOM
          What do you mean?

                    DOLORES
          I mean. I thought, when we met, that
          time, you know, that . . . But . . . I
          suppose it was just part of the act really.

87c.   EXT. CASTLE GROUNDS

O'MALLEY and MARY sit near a maze. They are listening with the
earpiece. They pull at it, each trying to get the best reception.

87d.   INT. GRAND BALLROOM DAY

TOM and DOLORES come into the grand ballroom.

                    TOM
          No wait, what do you mean?

                    DOLORES
          Between you and me. What I felt. When
          we sang. It was all just part of the ruse.

                    TOM
          No, I . . .

                    DOLORES
          Because if it was, it's a horrible gift that
          you have.

                    TOM
          I know.

                    DOLORES
          To be able to cast that kind of spell. That
          night I just lay in bed thinking about
          you. And would I see you again. What
          an idiot!

                    TOM
          No listen, I . . . I felt it too. I'm the idiot.
          You have no idea.

TOM and DOLORES stand looking at each other. She turns away and idly
picks up the remote control. Music begins to play. The drapes close. The
mirrorball spins.

87e.   EXT. CASTLE GROUNDS DAY

O'MALLEY and MARY are listening.

> O'MALLEY
> What's going on?

MARY smiles at him.

> O'MALLEY
> What's going on? Why doesn't he say
> his cue? My balls swole as big as
> grapefruit. Is that so difficult to
> remember?

87f.   INT. BALLROOM DAY

TOM approaches DOLORES. They take each other in their arms. They
begin to dance.

87g   EXT. CASTLE GROUNDS DAY

> O'MALLEY
> What the fuck is going on? Talk about
> your balls! Why isn't he talking about
> his bollocks?

> MARY
> He's in love, Mr O'Malley.

> O'MALLEY
> Love?! What about me?! I'll give him
> love!

> MARY
> No! Wait!

She grabs the detonator and runs off into the maze.

> O'MALLEY
> (pursuing her)
> What are you doing? Give me that!!

87h.   SPLIT SCREEN INT. BALLROOM / EXT. CASTLE GROUNDS DAY

On the left we have an aerial view of the maze. MARY runs around
through the maze with the detonator. O'MALLEY runs around in circles
after her. On the right TOM and DOLORES dance. They are about to kiss.
O'MALLEY catches MARY. They struggle and he grabs the detonator and
runs off out of the maze, chased by MARY. They run out of shot.

                    TOM
        I want to tell you. Everything. I'm not . . .
        who I seem . . .

TOM's blood explodes everywhere. He cries out in agony and surprise.
DOLORES screams. Squibs keep on detonating. There's absolutely loads
of them.

                    TOM
                 (whispers)
        Fucking hell, that's . . . sore . . .

DOLORES crouches down beside TOM. She presses the remote – the
music, stops the drapes open.

                  DOLORES
        Are you . . . are you shot?

                    TOM
                 (winded)
        You don't . . . understand . . .

                  DOLORES
        Don't move . . . Don't move . . .

She holds him. He reaches up holding her hand.

                  DOLORES
        I'm going to get help.

                    TOM
        No, don't . . .

                  DOLORES
        Just don't move, Clive. I'll be back. Just
        stay there. Just don't try to move.

DOLORES takes out her mobile phone.

                  DOLORES
        There's no fucking signal in here. Let
        me get someone. I'll be back.

                    TOM
        No, wait . . .

He tries to hang on to her, but she runs out. O'MALLEY bursts in another
door, followed by MARY. He quickly attacks TOM, dragging him to his feet.

                  O'MALLEY
        You . . . twit! What are you doing?

                    TOM
        This is wrong . . .

O'MALLEY

You're losing your mind! You can't drop
me in it, Tom, I won't let you!

MARY and TOM stare at the apoplectic O'MALLEY.

89.   EXT. BEACH DAY

DOLORES is rowing away from the island.

90.   INT. DRESSING ROOM NIGHT

TOM helps O'MALLEY put his hump on. TOM is downcast.

STAGE MANAGER
(over tannoy)
Ladies and gentlemen five minutes.
That's five minutes.

O'MALLEY
(warming up his voice)
Me me me me.

Go, Lovel, with all speed to Doctor Shaw;
Go thou to Friar Penkar. Bid them both meet me
Within this hour at Baynard's Castle

(Agitated To TOM.) What's the matter
with you? Clive is dead. Our troubles
are over. You're like one of Macbeth's
bloody witches.

TOM
You don't care? I mean, Dolores, I . . .

O'MALLEY
She wouldn't like you. Although I think
in spite of herself, she took a bit of a
shine to Clive, didn't she?

TOM
And we killed him.

O'MALLEY
Oh don't bore me with second thoughts,
Tom. You should be proud of yourself.
You are an actor.

They go out to the backstage area and make their way to the wings where
the show is about to begin.

TOM
You don't care, even a little bit? How she
must feel?

                    O'MALLEY
She's tough as old boots, that kid.
Anyway she always has my shoulder
to cry on.

                    TOM
You?

                    O'MALLEY
I know her longer than you.

                    TOM
So?

                    O'MALLEY
I know how she . . . feels.

                    TOM
How does she feel?

                    O'MALLEY
She . . . worships me.

TOM stands there in disbelief as O'MALLEY walks out on to the stage.

                    O'MALLEY
              (calling back up to him)
Our troubles are over!

TOM follows O'MALLEY as the curtain goes up.

                    O'MALLEY
Now is the winter . . .

91.   INT. BEDROOM NIGHT

TOM sits on MARY'S bed telling her a story.

                    TOM
When I first began acting, in Dublin,
me and some friends had a little theatre
company. We did shows for kids. And
one day we did a little play on the beach
in Dollymount. And one guy pretended
to be a blind man. He said, 'I'm blind.'
And all the kids said ' 'Can you see the
sea?' And he said, 'What's the sea?' And
they said, 'It's blue.' And he said.
'What's blue?' You know?

He smiles. MARY chuckles . . .

                    TOM
And then I came out and I said, 'I am
the saint of the beach. I can do anything

you want!' And the kids all started
jumping up and down, saying 'Make
him see!' So I said okay. And I said a
few things. and I put some water on his
eyes, and he goes, 'I can see! I can see!''
And the kids just basically went bananas,
at how brilliant this was. And when the
play was over we were packing up all
the stuff and the costumes. And this
little girl came over and said that her
brother was blind. And would I go and
make him see too? And I said that it
was only a play. And I wasn't really the
saint of the beach. And she said, 'But
you made him see.' And I . . . tried to
explain it. But I just became . . . very
tired. And I was just putting the stuff in
the van with this little girl at my heels.
And I . . . pretended I couldn't hear her.
You know? And I feel like that again
now.

> MARY

Uncle Tommy?

He looks at her. She pulls back the bedclothes, puts her slippers on.

> MARY
> You're too good for your own good.

92.   INT. COCK AND WEATHERVANE NIGHT

The bar is closed. O'MALLEY sits with BARRELLER and DOLORES at the
bar. RONNIE and LESLEY play pool in a corner. O'MALLEY is drunk.

> DOLORES
> And when I got back he'd vanished. His
> blood was everywhere but he was gone.
> I mean. I'm the one. I must have led his
> killers to him. I'm so sorry Mr O'Malley. I
> feel terrible.

> BARRELLER
> I should never have let you go. I mean
> he robbed me, And left me in the shitter.
> But to be killed like that.

> O'MALLEY
> If only I hadn't let slip our conversation
> about the money.

                    BARRELLER
         You weren't to know. I should've kept
         my big mouth shut.

                    O'MALLEY
         Clive and I were never too close,
         Dolores. He had many qualities about
         him, which to tell you the truth made
         him something of an insect.

The phone in the bar rings. Ronnie picks it up.

                    DOLORES
         Everyone does stupid things.

                    BARRELLER
         That's right. We do.

                    RONNIE
         Dolores . . .

DOLORES goes to the phone.

                    O'MALLEY
         No, Barreller, not all of us. I'm sorry to
         contradict you. But not all of us. I need a
         piss.

O'MALLEY stumbles off out the toilet.

93.   INT. RITA'S HOUSE NIGHT / INT. BAR NIGHT

                    DOLORES
         Hello?

TOM and MARY sit at the bottom of the stairs in Rita's house.

                    MARY
         Bonjour. I'm ringing from the Serious
         Injury Hospital. We have a gentleman
         here who's been asking for you. He's
         been shot.

                    DOLORES
         Clive?

                    MARY
         Yes. Clive.

                    DOLORES
         That can't be. I saw him. He was shot
         about twenty times.

                        89

Suddenly there's a loud banging at the shutters of the pub. BARRELLER looks at RONNIE and LESLEY. They look at BARRELLER, BARRELLER shouts out.

> BARRELLER
>
> We're closed!

> MARY
>
> We have the best surgeons in the world here. There's nothing we haven't seen.

> DOLORES
>
> Yes, of course . . .

> MARY
>
> He's still in a very serious condition, but a visit from you, I think would brighten his spirits considerably.

The banging continues.

> BARRELLER
>
> We're closed!

> DOLORES
>
> You're certain it's him. That he's alive . . .

> MARY
>
> How many people called Clive do you think were shot in Tubbetstown Castle and have your number?

> DOLORES
>
> No. I'm sorry. Could I see him tomorrow, do you think?

> MARY
> (looking at TOM)
> I think he . . . he'd like that very much.

DOLORES hangs up. She stands there thoughtfully.

The banging continues.

> BARRELLER
>
> Jesus, Ronnie, see who it is. Tell them to fuck off.

94.   INT. COCK AND WEATHERVANE NIGHT

RONNIE opens the door. JOCK attacks him and grabs the pool cue. LESLEY goes to help and JOCK hits him with the cue. JOCK has RONNIE in a grip around the neck, and he brandishes a pool cue with the other hand. LESLEY sits on the floor holding his head. BARRELLER holds his hands out, placatory. DOLORES stands there shocked.

JOCK

The Aran Islands is fucking freezing!

BARRELLER

What?

JOCK

How many Barrellers are in your fucking
outfit?!

BARRELLER

I'm Barreller. I'm the only Barreller!

JOCK
(hits RONNIE)
Is this Barreller? (Hits RONNIE again.)
Hey you! Is this Barreller.

BARRELLER

Hey! Go easy. That's his . . . he has a
bad ear.

DOLORES
. . . That's his bad ear . . .

JOCK

I'll give him two fucking bad ears! (He
hits RONNIE again.)

LESLEY goes to help RONNIE. JOCK smacks LESLEY with the pool cue.
LESLEY recoils.

O'MALLEY hearing the commotion peeps out the toilet door. He doesn't
like what's happening. He quietly shuts the door.

BARRELLER

Here! That's enough! He's not the full
shilling!

BARRELLER attacks JOCK. JOCK drops RONNIE, who sinks to the floor.
JOCK swings the cue at BARRELLER. BARRELLER catches the cue and
sweeps JOCK'S feet from under him. JOCK hits the floor hard. BARRELLER
sits on JOCK'S back, holding his head to the floor.

BARRELLER

Who are you? What do want?

JOCK

Where's Magnani's money?

BARRELLER

I gave it to Clive.

JOCK

Who is Clive?

91

                    BARRELLER
The guy your people killed in
Tubbetstown.

                    JOCK
I've never been down to Tubble . . .
town! Who sent me to the Aran Islands?

                    BARRELLER
I have no idea what you're talking
about. Who was the Scottish bloke who
came here?

                    JOCK
What Scottish bloke? I'm the Scottish
bloke!

                    BARRELLER
Then who the fuck is Jock?

                    JOCK
I'm Jock!

                    BARRELLER
Do you like popcorn?

                    JOCK
What?

BARRELLER bashes his head on the floor.

                    DOLORES
Dad, be careful . . .

                    BARRELLER
Do you eat popcorn?

                    JOCK
I can't. I'm allergic to Popcorn. Now, for
the last time. Where's Magnani's
money?

                    BARRELLER
I gave it to Clive!!!

                    JOCK
There isn't any Clive!

                    BARRELLER
She saw him! Dolores! tell this fucking
eejit what happened to Clive.

                    DOLORES
He's . . . He was killed.

                    92

                          JOCK
              Look. That's it. Let me up please.

BARRELLER lets JOCK up.

                          JOCK
              Do you have the money?

                          BARRELLER
No.

                          JOCK
              Alright. I don't know what sort of
              fucking pantomime is going on here.
              But you've brought it on yourself
              Magnani's coming over.

                          BARRELLER
              Let him come. Her.

                          BARRELLER
              Who's her?

                          JOCK
              Magnani. She's a woman!! (He's had
              enough.) For fuck's sake!

JOCK leaves. DOLORES nurses RONNIE.

                          BARRELLER
              Let her come then. What can I do? Let
              her come. Clive's dead, what can I do?

DOLORES looks up at BARRELLER.

95.   INT. TOILET NIGHT

O'MALLEY is scrabbling out a little window.

96.   EXT. LANEWAY NIGHT

O'MALLEY hits the pavement and gets up, terrifiedly scampering down
the lane.

97.   EXT. TAXI RANK DAY

DOLORES gets into a taxi.

She is being watched from behind a newspaper. It's JOCK. He folds it and
approaches a taxi.

                          JOCK
              Follow that taxi. She's ma auntie. I'm her
              uncle.

                          93

98.   EXT. GATE TO GROUNDS OF SERIOUS INJURY HOSPITAL DAY

There is a turnstile in the wall. DOLORES goes through it.

99.   EXT. GROUNDS OF SERIOUS INJURY HOSPITAL DAY

TOM disguised as CLIVE sits in a wheelchair. His upper body is encased in plaster. Some other PATIENTS have also been wheeled out to take the sun. NURSES attend them. DOLORES sits with him on a bench.

                    TOM
          I know. I was extremely lucky. You see
          most of the bullets hit me in . . . the
          arse.

                    DOLORES
          Why is all this plaster around your
          chest?

                    TOM
          Em. A lot of them went up my arse. Into
          the chest . . . ular area.

                    DOLORES
          My God.

                    TOM
          Doctors never seen anything like it.

                    DOLORES
          Clive. I'm glad you survived. But do you
          have the money?

                    TOM
          If I knew where it was I'd tell you, I swear,
          but my would-be assassins, whoever
          they be, got their hands on it. I really
          want to make it up to you, I do. And I'm
          going to work every hour God sends me
          until you have it again.

DOLORES looks down forlornly.

                    TOM
          But the reason I needed to see you is
          because I, and you have every reason to
          reject me, but I . . .

                    DOLORES
          I know. You don't have to say anything.
          I have feelings too.

TOM looks at her hopefully.

94

                    DOLORES
        But they're for someone else.

                    TOM
        Who . . . ?

                    DOLORES
        He's an actor I don't know that well. But
        I know I could love him.

                    TOM
        Is he . . . a good actor?

                    DOLORES
        He's wonderful. It's your cousin, Clive.
        It's Anthony O'Malley.

TOM gags. He begins to choke. DOLORES helps him by banging the
plaster on his back violently. He falls out of the chair. He recovers.
DOLORES helps him into the chair again.

                    DOLORES
        I don't ever want to see you again, Clive.
        You've caused so much misery.

She leaves. TOM watches her go. He is about to get up, when a pair of
hands suddenly grab the wheelchair. It's JOCK.

                    JOCK
        Alright my fucking bucko!

TOM struggles.

                    TOM
        What do you want? Get off me!

                    JOCK
        The famous Clive!

                    TOM
        No you've got the wrong man.

JOCK has handcuffs, he is trying to handcuff himself to TOM, but can't get
the other cuff around TOM'S plaster cast. They are struggling.

                    JOCK
        Tell it to Magnani.

From across the grounds, NURSES watch JOCK apparently abusing a
cripple, they run over shouting at JOCK. JOCK gets the other handcuff
around the arm of the wheelchair. And runs pushing TOM through the
grounds.

                    JOCK
        I always get my man . . . I have to admit
        it was a nice touch getting your

                    95

accomplice to imitate Barreller. The
Aran Islands. Nice. But the fun's over
Clive. Magnani arrives tonight for her
money. And for you. And for Barreller for
being so fucking stupid with his big
fucking mouth. And for that bitch who
told me you were dead.

                    TOM
She thought I was dead.

                    JOCK
Save it for the interrogation. Midnight.
Our good friend Barreller's office.

He rattles the handcuff on the wheelchair.

                    JOCK
I trust you'll be joining us. (He laughs.)
Here, just for my own curiosity. Who
shot you?

                    TOM
A jealous lover.

                    JOCK
Are you kidding me? You're not worth a
bullet.

JOCK produces a knife.

                    JOCK
I've got other ideas for you. What do you
think?

JOCK loosens his shirt to reveal a necklace of shrivelled human ears.
TOM shrieks and leaps out of the wheelchair and through the turnstile.

                    JOCK
What the fuck!!

JOCK tries to follow by leaping into the turnstile but is restrained by the
wheelchair which gets stuck in the turnstile behind him as TOM emerges.
The turnstile jams. JOCK frantically reaches for his keys to unlock himself,
but fumbles them. He tries a key. It's the wrong one. He pulls it out
sharply and the keys fly out of his hand. They drop beyond his reach.
JOCK is trapped.

                    JOCK
Will someone please get me out of here?!

100.   EXT. STREET EVENING

TOM frantically bashes himself against a wall, cracking the plaster on his body, trying to get it off. PASSERS BY stare at him.

> TOM
> Doctor's orders. It comes off today.

101.   EXT. TAXI RANK DAY

JOCK runs to the taxis, still handcuffed to the wheelchair. He hails a taxi.

> JOCK
> The airport. Arrivals.

102.   INT. THEATRE NIGHT

The play is just starting. The CAST are assembled for O'MALLEY'S first speech.

> O'MALLEY
> Now is the winter of our discontent
> Made glorious summer by this son of York;
> And all the clouds that lour'd upon our house
> In the deep bosom of the ocean buried.

TOM runs on stage in a half-arsed costume and smashes O'MALLEY with a big sword. O'MALLEY is winded. He sinks to his knees. The cast look on aghast as TOM finishes the play which has only been on for a few seconds.

> TOM
> God and your arms be praised,
> victorious friends! The day is ours, the
> bloody dog is dead.

The STAGE MANAGER frantically flicks to the end of the script and says 'curtain' into her headset. The curtain descends to genial puzzlement and a smattering of baffled applause. Onstage TOM drags O'MALLEY to the wings.

> O'MALLEY
> What are you doing?

> TOM
> We don't have time. Magnani's coming.
> Give me the money or we're all fucked.

103.   INT. AIRPORT ARRIVALS NIGHT

TRAVELLERS are coming through to the concourse. A couple of hard-looking well dressed HOODS come and stand at the sliding doors. checking the joint. They see JOCK and acknowledge him. One of the HOODS signals behind him. We see a pair of stockinged high-heeled legs come through. She stops. We don't see her face. JOCK nods weakly and swallows. The entourage move out.

104.   INT. DRESSING ROOM NIGHT

TOM pushes O'MALLEY into the dressing room, and pulls the place apart looking for the money.

> O'MALLEY
> Have you lost your tiny mind? This is Shakespeare! This is the theatre! The people need us.

> TOM
> Where's the money?

> O'MALLEY
> We're their moral barometer! All over Dublin tonight it'll be bedlam! You can't stop a play!

TOM grabs O'MALLEY and looks him in the eye.

> TOM
> A certain party owed money by another certain party neither party having ever met. You know what happens if they meet? They give and get information. All we have is that. We control the information. If we don't, one of those parties is going to come down here and cut your little mickey off. And I'm this close to not caring any more. Where's the money?

O'MALLEY nips open his Richard III hump to reveal the money. TOM quickly gathers it.

> TOM
> Now, go next door, swallow your pride and borrow a dress.

105.   INT. CELLARS OF THE COCK NIGHT

BARRELLER comes down the spiral staircase alone, lit by the street lamps outside the window. He rehearses his spiel, he is nervous.

> BARRELLER
> We are both, are we not, business people? I have been reasonable! But who expects to be tricked? I'm . . . at . . . a loss . . .

We see that he is alone, rehearsing for MAGNANI. The windows are at pavement level. Headlamps sweep the room. A car comes to a halt. He hears footsteps. A pair of high heels pass the window. They come down the outside stair to a door which swings open, backlighting a glamorous looking WOMAN and a MAN in a trilby hat. The WOMAN'S voice is low and breathless.

                    WOMAN / O'MALLEY
Mr Barreller . . . ?

                    BARRELLER
Just Barreller is fine.

                    WOMAN / O'MALLEY
Well. We've had a fine time, haven't we?

                    BARRELLER
I was fooled Ms Magnani. I was tricked
I was . . .

                    WOMAN / O'MALLEY
We've recovered the money. And we
have the culprit.

                    BARRELLER
Clive . . . ?

                    WOMAN / O'MALLEY
I have a very effective Scottish friend.

                    BARRELLER
But Clive is dead.

                    WOMAN / O'MALLEY
He's seems to fool you very easily. But
I don't like being tricked. We're bringing
him here tonight. I thought you might
like to watch.

                    BARRELLER
Watch what?

                    WOMAN
The fun.

                    BARRELLER
I . . . don't think I do.

                    WOMAN
It's not for everybody. Perhaps you
might like to retire somewhere.

BARRELLER hesitates. The MAN / TOM pulls out his big sword and smashes the single light bulb.

                    MAN / TOM
                 (like one of the Krays)
Don't worry. We'll tidy up afterwards.
You won't even know we were here.

                        BARRELLER
            Oh God . . .

BARRELLER goes to the door.

                        WOMAN
            Cheer up. It's over.

BARRELLER leaves, heavy hearted.

                        TOM
            That was pretty fucking good, Tony.

                        O'MALLEY
                  (with false modesty)
            Well I . . . (Snapping out of it.) What do
            you mean?

                        TOM
            I mean that was very good.

                        O'MALLEY
            But what are you saying?

                        TOM
            What do you mean?

                        O'MALLEY
            I mean, are you trying to say . . . I'm,
            you know . . . because I'm not.

TOM is fixing O'MALLEY'S wig and watching out the window.

                        TOM
            Oh for fuck's sake! Yes! I think you're
            gay! I think you like big hairy men!
            I think you're a degenerate!

                        O'MALLEY
            Oh it's all coming out now.

Out the window TOM sees a long white limo pull up, followed by another
car with MAGNANI'S HOODS.

                        O'MALLEY
            All the jealousy, all the spite.

                        TOM
            Look, you're on, just go.

TOM is pushing O'MALLEY out.

                        O'MALLEY
            Well I'm sorry to tell you, you've just
            made a powerful enemy, my boy.

                          100

                    TOM
        I'm not your boy. Just get out, get out,
        whatever, Jesus.

                  O'MALLEY
        This is not the end of this! We are so
        very, very far from the end.

                    TOM
             (stares at O'MALLEY)
        . . . right.

106.   EXT. STREET NIGHT

O'MALLEY, approaches the limo. JOCK is walking around the limo to open
a rear door for the occupant. The windows are tinted, we can't see inside.
JOCK stops. The HOODS loiter at another car.

                    JOCK
        Who are you?

                  O'MALLEY
        I'm Mrs O'Growney, I represent . . .
        Barreller.

                    JOCK
        You represent him?

                  O'MALLEY
        I have your money.

JOCK considers.

                    JOCK
        Get in.

JOCK opens a rear door and O'MALLEY climbs in.

107.   INT. BARRELLER'S OFFICE NIGHT

TOM watches the cars depart. He bends to pick up a bag at the foot of the
spiral staircase. A drop of liquid splashes on the back of his neck. He
looks up, another drop and then another on his face. And then a whole
containerful of liquid splashes all over him.

                    TOM
        What the fuck!

He is soaked, staring up into the shadows in the eves.

                    TOM
        Who's there?

                      101

An empty fuel can clatters to the floor. TOM looks at it. At the top of the spiral staircase a figure lights a zippo lighter. A woman's voice, sensual, dangerous.

> WOMAN
> I wouldn't move if I were you. Things
> might become heated

> TOM
> Who are you?

The figure descends the staircase slowly. A beautiful woman, sunglasses, long hair.

> WOMAN
> Oh . . . You disappoint me. And you
> were doing so well. Mr Quirk.

> TOM
> How do you know me?

> WOMAN
> There's very little I don't know or can't
> find out.

She steps off the staircase.

> WOMAN
> I'm Magnani.

> TOM
> You're Magnani? Then (He signals to the
> window.) Who, where?

> WOMAN
> Don't panic, my love . . .

She moves towards him, lighter in hand. She throws him some handcuffs.

> WOMAN
> Recognise these? Please attach yourself
> to the window.

He places the handcuffs through a bar in the window and cuffs himself now facing out the window with his back to her.

> WOMAN
> Tighter. You've been a very bold boy.

He painfully closes the cuffs tighter on himself

> WOMAN
> (approvingly)
> Mm. You know what you deserve.

She comes close, holding the Zippo near his face.

                    WOMAN
          I think you secretly want to be
          punished, don't you?

She presses close against him.

                    WOMAN
          You feel terrible. The weight of the pain
          you've caused. You're a bad bad person.

She kisses his neck, his ear.

                    WOMAN
          You're shaking. You're trembling.

                    TOM
          1 . . . I've never been tortured before.

                    WOMAN
          No?

She bites his ear, painfully.

                    TOM
          Ahh . . . (He hisses.)

                    WOMAN
          I think you like it. I think this is what
          you wanted. To be caught. To be
          trapped. To be made to suffer. Well. Here
          you are . . . Tell me you deserve to be
          punished.

                    TOM
          Huh?

She slaps him.

                    TOM
          I deserve to be punished.

She slaps him.

                    WOMAN
          Say 'I want you to hurt me.'

                    TOM
          Eh but I . . .

She slaps him. Hard.

                    TOM
          I . . . I want you to hurt me.

                    DOLORES
          I will.

She kisses him. Tenderly. TOM doesn't know what the fuck is happening. She begins to kiss him with more passion. He can't help responding. They are locked in a desperate kiss. They part. Panting.

The WOMAN removes her disguise. It's DOLORES.

> DOLORES
>
> Not bad . . .

> TOM
>
> Dolores! What are you . . .

108.   EXT. COAST ROAD NIGHT

The moonlight sparkles off the water. MAGNANI'S car drives along. Her HOODS follow in a second car.

109.   INT. CAR NIGHT

O'MALLEY in the car with MAGNANI. She is absolutely gorgeous. They drive along by the sea. He can't help ogling her breasts.

> MAGNANI
>
> So, Mrs O'Growney, as a woman, which do you think instils more respect among men, the fear of violence or the dim and distant promise of sexual intercourse?

> O'MALLEY
>
> I wouldn't know . . . The . . . sex?

> MAGNANI
>
> My feelings precisely. So you found the culprit?

> O'MALLEY
>
> (uncomfortable under her gaze)
> Well, not me. I'm little more than a secretary. Turn left here.

110.   INT. BARRELLER'S OFFICE NIGHT

TOM is still cuffed. DOLORES smokes a cigarette. She put one in TOM S mouth and goes to light it with her zippo. TOM flinches.

> DOLORES
>
> Relax. It's water, You know, you had me?
> Right up to where you blew yourself up.

> TOM
>
> Too much?

DOLORES

A tad . . . And then telling me he'd
survived

TOM

I . . . wanted to see you again . . .

DOLORES

Why? To gloat?

TOM

No! No! I regretted it from the word go.
I wish we never did it.

DOLORES

You know. You're a fucking good actor.

TOM

(snorts)

I'm a thief, Dolores. But we're giving the
money back. O'Malley's with Magnani
now. And I know this mightn't be the
time. I mean we can discuss this later,
but I need to go and make sure he's
alright.

DOLORES

Perhaps he has what's coming to him.

TOM

I thought you said you loved him

DOLORES

Are you out of your fucking mind? He's
the biggest arsehole I've ever met. Let's
let him suffer.

TOM looks at her. Can she really be this hard?

111.   INT. LIMO NIGHT

O'MALLEY sits opposite MAGNANI. He feels awkward, he tries smiling at
MAGNANI, but she, behind her sunglasses, seems inscrutable, if, so far,
benign.

MAGNANI

I hope you don't mind me saying Mrs
O'Growney, but you are a most unusual
figure of a woman.

O'MALLEY squirms with embarrassment and wounded pride. He becomes
catty.

105

> O'MALLEY

Not all of us are blessed with outward beauty, Ms Magnani. Then again, it's a shallow measure by which to judge, I find.

The atmosphere becomes frosty.

> O'MALLEY

Besides. It . . . fades. (Looking out the window.) 'What a piece of work is a man. How noble in reason. How infinite in faculties . . . In action how like an angel . . . the beauty of the world. The paragon of animals. And yet to me, what is this quintessence of dust? Man . . .'

> MAGNANI

'Man delights not me – no, nor woman either, though by your smiling you seem to say so.'

> O'MALLEY

You know . . . your Shakespeare.

> MAGNANI

Never blindly equate beauty with stupidity, Mrs O'Growney. It's a . . . dangerous assumption.

O'MALLEY coughs awkwardly, and smiles weakly.

112.   O'MALLEY'S OLD HOUSE NIGHT

The windows are boarded up. There is a 'For Sale' sign. The Limo pulls up. O'MALLEY gets out. JOCK gets out. Some of the HOODS get out.

> MAGNANI

Is this your house?

> O'MALLEY

It's one of Barreller's.

> MAGNANI

One of? I like that.

113.   INT. O'MALLEY'S OLD HOUSE NIGHT

O'MALLEY leads MAGNANI and JOCK into the living room. There is now no furniture. O'MALLEY then goes to the big fireplace and sticks his arm up, feeling around in the chimney.

> MAGNANI

What are you doing?

                            O'MALLEY
        He left it up here.

                            JOCK
        Let me have a look.

                            O'MALLEY
        I have it. It's just caught.

O'MALLEY takes a box of matches from the fireplace and lights one,
sticking his head up the chimney to get the money. His voice echoes up
the chimney.

                            O'MALLEY
        I have it.

He emerges from the chimney with a bag. JOCK takes it and examines the
contents. Smoke is beginning to billow from O'MALLEY'S head.

                            MAGNANI
        Mrs O'Growney.

                            O'MALLEY
        Yes?

                            MAGNANI
        Your hair is on fire.

O'MALLEY reaches up. He burns his hand. He pulls the wig off. His
glasses and earrings also fly off. He throws the wig into the fireplace. He
freezes. He has no disguise.

                            O'MALLEY
        Em. I'm just going to run to the
        bathroom.

JOCK grabs him.

                            JOCK
        Wait a minute. You're a bloke.

                            O'MALLEY
        No, I'm . . . young man . . . please.

JOCK rips at O'MALLEY'S clothes.

                            JOCK
        He's a bloke! Are you wearing a wire?

                            O'MALLEY
        No. No.

                            MAGNANI
        Who are you? What are you doing?

O'MALLEY
Just . . . take your money. That's what
you wanted. Just take it.

MAGNANI
Are you the police?

O'MALLEY
No! No, no.

JOCK
Who are you?

JOCK pins O'MALLEY to the floor.

O'MALLEY
I'm . . . an actor.

JOCK
What?

O'MALLEY
Please. Just take your money.

MAGNANI
Where's Barreller? Are you Barreller?

O'MALLEY
No. But it doesn't matter! Surely it
doesn't matter now!

MAGNANI
No, you see, Mrs O'Growney, it does
matter.

JOCK produces a hatchet.

O'MALLEY
What's that for? You don't need that. You
have your money. Let's not do anything
stupid.

JOCK
You already have.

JOCK smashes the hatchet into the floor inches from O'MALLEY'S nose.

MAGNANI
Who are you?

O'MALLEY
I'm an actor. My name is Anthony
O'Malley. I'm in a production of Richard
III. The man who robbed you. His name
. . . is Tommy Quirk. He's in the play too.

You can get him there. We're on tomorrow
night. It's the last night of the show. You
can . . . get him. Please. I didn't do it.
Look in my handbag. Please.

JOCK looks at MAGNANI. She nods to him. He empties O'MALLEY's
handbag. There's a playbill of Richard III. JOCK has a look and hands it to
MAGNANI. She has a look. The photo of O'MALLEY is from many years
ago and very vain.

O'MALLEY

Tommy Quirk. At the back.

MAGNANI looks at TOM'S picture.

O'MALLEY

That's him.

A blue police light sweeps the room. A siren wails. JOCK takes MAGNANI
and leads her out the back through the patio doors. O'MALLEY gets up,
drained. He goes to the window.

114.   EXT. STREET NIGHT

O'MALLEY'S POV. DOLORES and TOM are getting out of BARRELLER'S
van. The blue light is flashing.

115.   INT. O'MALLEY'S OLD HOUSE NIGHT

O'MALLEY leans against the wall. He looks at the programme on the floor.
The pages blow in the wind from the patio doors. TOM'S picture. O'MALLEY
closes his eyes as TOM begins banging on the door. Calling to O'MALLEY
to see if he's alright.

116.   EXT. THEATRE NIGHT

It's almost showtime. PUNTERS come towards the theatre. There is a sign
which says, 'Final Performance'.

117.   INT. DRESSING ROOM NIGHT

TOM is getting ready. His spirits are high. O'MALLEY sits dejectedly,
sickened with fear and his own cowardice. He takes a lash of whiskey.

TOM

What's the matter with you? The
money?

O'MALLEY

exhales heavily through his nose.

TOM

Well. I'm relieved. No money is worth
that kind of hassle Tony. From now on?

109

I'm just gonna . . . appreciate everything.
Jesus, Dolores is something else, isn't
she? Laughing at us all that time, letting
us carry on with our plan. She's
something else.

118.   INT. FOYER NIGHT

MAGNANI and JOCK distribute tickets to a dozen besuited HOODS,

119.   EXT. STAGE DOOR NIGHT

Two HOODS take position at the stage door.

120.   INT. FOYER NIGHT

MARY meets DOLORES

> MARY
> Hello, I'm Mary. I'm nine. My uncle's in
> this play. He's a very good man,

> DOLORES
> Oh, right. I'm Dolores . . . How are you?

> MARY
> Generally, a bit disappointed usually.
> Let's sit together.

> DOLORES
> Okay.

They make their way in.

> MARY
> You're incredibly beautiful. Did you
> know that?

> DOLORES
> Oh, thank you.

> MARY
> Don't be shy. It's true. Wait 'til you see
> my uncle. He's a terrific actor. I tend to
> speak my mind. I develop in public.
> I evolve quite openly.

121.   INT. DRESSING ROOM NIGHT

TOM and O'MALLEY sit waiting. The STAGE MANAGER announces 'Five
minutes to curtain. Five minutes please. Best of luck.' TOM pipes up.

TOM

> Listen. I think it's only fair to tell you. . . .
> I'm meeting her for a drink later. I know
> you like her. I mean I don't know if it's
> ever going to amount to anything. But
> I wanted you to know. She's going to be
> in tonight. And I'll tell you. It's making
> me nervous as fuck,

O'MALLEY just looks at him.

122. INT. THEATRE NIGHT

MAGNANI and her HOODS take up a whole row. JOCK passes programmes
down to all of them. They all open the programmes to the page with
TOM'S picture.

123. INT. THEATRE NIGHT

DOLORES and MARY come into the theatre from the foyer. An USHER
points out their seat.

124. INT. THEATRE NIGHT

O'MALLEY onstage. Opening soliloquy. He reclines on a chaise longue.
HELGA massages his shoulders. ACTOR 2 carries a drinks tray.

O'MALLEY

> (as Richard, Duke of Gloucester)
> Plots have I laid, inductions dangerous,
> By drunken prophecies, libels and dreams
> To set my brother Clarence and the King
> In deadly hate, the one against the other:
> And if King Edward be as true and just
> As I am subtle, false, and treacherous,
> This day should Clarence closely be mew'd up
> About a prophecy, which says that 'G'
> Of Edward's heirs the murderer shall be
> Dive, thoughts, down to my soul: here Clarence
>   comes.

Enter CLARENCE, guarded, by five goose-steppers. One of whom is TOM.
He carries a large eagle standard.

125. INT. THEATRE STALLS NIGHT

MAGNANI, JOCK and the HOODS register TOM. Perhaps one or two little
nudges. JOCK leans over and whispers to MAGNANI. She nods.

111

126.   INT. THEATRE ONSTAGE NIGHT

The scene continues. TOM is scanning the theatre for DOLORES. He sees her sitting with MARY. He gives her a little smile.

> O'MALLEY
> (as Richard)
> Brother, good day; what means this armed guard
> That waits upon your grace?

> CLARENCE
> His Majesty,
> Tend'ring my person's safety, hath appointed
> This conduct to convey me to the Tower.

> O'MALLEY
> Upon what cause?

O'MALLEY does a sweeping hand gesture. TOM wiggles his fingers to give DOLORES a little wave. The standard slips away from him.

> CLARENCE
> Because my name is George.

The top of the standard strikes a WOMAN in the front row on the top of her head and smashes. She stands, clutching her hair. A MAN comes to her assistance. TOM goes to retrieve the standard, making apologetic hand gestures. O'MALLEY tries to continue the scene.

> O'MALLEY
> Alack, my lord, that fault is none of yours:
> He should for that commit your godfathers.
> O, belike his Majesty hath some intent
> That you should be new-christen'd in the Tower . . .

The HOODS in the audience are sniggering behind their hands. While TOM, completely out of character, is whispering at the side of the stage, inquiring after the WOMAN.

127.   EXT. STAGE DOOR

The two HOODS outside the stage door stamp their feet, and smoke, trying to keep warm. One HOOD idly takes a knuckleduster from his coat pocket and slips it on, clenching his fist, practising.

128.   INT. THEATRE NIGHT

Act II sc. iii. Enter one CITIZEN at one door. ANOTHER at the other. Refugees flee with their belongings.

> CITIZEN 1
> (laughing with husband)
> Good morrow, neighbour: whither away so fast?

CITIZEN 1
(laughing with husband)
I promise you, I scarcely know myself. Hear you
the news abroad?

129.   INT. WINGS / BACKSTAGE NIGHT

TOM is in the wings about to come out of his dressing room and excuses
himself past two HOODS waiting, he doesn't know who they are.

TOM
Sorry, excuse me.

He passes two more HOODS in the wings.

CITIZEN 1
(laughing)
Yes, that the King is dead.

CITIZEN 2
(crying)
Ill news, by'rlady; seldom comes the better.
I fear, I fear, 'twill prove a giddy world.

Enter TOM as CITIZEN 3. Needless to say, he is just awful. He has a
strange accent, and appears unsure of himself. He nearly trips over his
costume.

TOM
Neighbours, God speed.

CITIZEN 1
Give you good morrow, sir.

TOM
Doth the news hold of good King Edward's death?

CITIZEN 2
Ay, sir, it is too true, God help the while.

TOM
Then, masters, look to see a troublous world.

CITIZEN 1
No, no; by God's good grace, his son shall reign.

There's a pause. It's Tom's line, but he's gone. He's dried. So . . .

TOM
Then, masters, look to see a troublous world.

The ACTOR playing CITIZEN 1 is a little confused, but gives TOM his cue
again.

CITIZEN 1
No, no; by God's good grace, his son shall reign

113

There is a long pause. The citizens laugh and cry again. TOM finally appears to have taken this in. He nods sagely, before saying with different emphasis and renewed vigour, gravely:

> TOM
>
> Then, masters, look to see a troublous world.
> I'm sorry. Line?!

MAGNANI, JOCK and the HOODS look on with morbid fascination. One or two checking TOM'S photograph in the programme.

DOLORES can hardly watch. MARY calls out his line.

> MARY
>
> Woe to that land that's governed by a child!

> TOM
>
> Oh yeah, sorry. What?

> MARY
>
> Woe to that land that's governed by a child!

> TOM
>
> Woe to that land that's governed by a child!
>
> Thanks Mary. Sorry everybody.

The CITIZENS laugh and cry. There is thunder and lightning.

130.   INT. THEATRE BACKSTAGE NIGHT

TOM exits into the wings. He bumps into O'MALLEY and past some HOODS. The HOODS hold bunches of flowers.

> TOM
>
> I'm having the worst show of my life.

> O'MALLEY
> (worriedly watching HOODS)
> Me too.

> TOM
> (looking at HOODS)
> Who are all these people?

> O'MALLEY
>
> . . . Well . . . wishers . . .

131.   INT. THEATRE NIGHT

Act V sc. iv. There's a battle scene. ACTORS fencing. Strobe lights and blood red background. They all freeze in a tableau and O'MALLEY enters and gives his all.

O'MALLEY

A horse! A horse! My kingdom for a horse!

CATESBY

Withdraw, my lord; I'll help you to a horse.

O'MALLEY

Slave! I have set my life upon a cast,
And I will stand the hazard of the die.
I think there be six Richmonds in the field:
Five have I slain instead of him.
A horse! A horse! My kingdom for a horse!

The stage breaks into action again. O'MALLEY exits and re-enters on the other side. RICHMOND enters and the stage again freezes to tableau. O'MALLEY and RICHMOND fence. It's a tightly choreographed nail-biter.

The HOODS all look on with rapt attention. The fight is good.

Onstage, O'MALLEY as Richard is finally slain.

132.   INT. THEATRE NIGHT

The final speech. The Cast are arranged in an arc across the stage. TOM stands as a soldier, extreme stage right. He's at the end of the arc at the lip of the stage.

RICHMOND

Abate the edge of traitors, gracious Lord,
That would reduce these bloody days again,
And make poor England weep in streams of blood.
Let them not live to taste this land's increase,
That would with treason wound this fair land's
    peace.
Now civil wounds are stopped; peace lives again.

The cast kneel, hands joined in prayer.

RICHMOND

That she may long live here, God say Amen.

ALL

Amen.

Their Nazi salutes become orthodox salutes. The lights dim. The curtain begins to descend. The audience applaud. But TOM being so far forward has lost his mark. The curtain hits against him and falls behind him, Leaving him alone on the stage. The Audience, but not MAGNANI and the HOODS laugh at him. He frantically tries to find his way back in. But the curtain raises for the cast curtain call. He awkwardly joins them. DOLORES is dying of embarrassment for TOM but can't help laughing.

115

133.   INT. DRESSING ROOM NIGHT

TOM takes a swig of O'MALLEY'S whiskey.

O'MALLEY comes in and clocks him but doesn't say anything. O'MALLEY
begins to undress.

> TOM
> (angry)
> Incredible. The worst yet. You'd think I
> couldn't get any worse. But, unbelievably,
> on the last night? I managed to find
> lower depths. God. It must be all the
> excitement. Tony? What do you think?

O'MALLEY doesn't answer.

> TOM
> Here. Let me help you.

TOM goes to O'MALLEY and begins to help him take his hump off. When
TOM touches O'MALLEY, O'MALLEY stiffens,

> O'MALLEY
> Tom . . .

> TOM
> Yeah?

There's a knock at the door.

> O'MALLEY
> I've betrayed you.

TOM pauses. There's more knocking at the door. O'MALLEY closes his
eyes.

> TOM
> What do you mean?

> O'MALLEY
> I'm weak, Tom.

> TOM
> Who's at the door?

> O'MALLEY
> Everything's so wrong.

The door opens. It's MAGNANI and JOCK. We see HOODS behind them,
blocking the door. JOCK shuts it behind him. MAGNANI carries a big
bunch of flowers. TOM takes a step backwards.

> MAGNANI
> Well. Gentlemen.

                    TOM

Tony . . .

                  O'MALLEY

This is Tommy Quirk.

                  MAGNANI

Yes. We saw your picture.

                    TOM

What do you want?

                  MAGNANI

We want the man who fooled everybody.

                  O'MALLEY
              (downhearted)

This is him.

                    TOM

Tony . . .

                  MAGNANI

Well . . . may I? . . .

She pours herself a nip of whiskey.

                  MAGNANI

This is where we have a little problem.
You're telling us he played all these
parts?

                  O'MALLEY

He did. And wonderfully.

                  MAGNANI

Mr O'Malley. We were at the show
tonight.

                  MAGNANI
              (she takes a drink)
And this is our problem.

                    JOCK

That fucker can't act!

                    TOM

Ah here. I might of had a bad show!
That can happen!

                    JOCK

You were shit! You got your lines wrong!
You stood in the wrong places! You
nearly brained a woman in the front
row!

                              TOM
                  I've been tired! I have good nights! Tony!

                            O'MALLEY
                  To be fair. On occasion. He has been
                  suff . . . iciently . . . okay.

                              TOM
                  Oh thanks, Tony. That's great . . . (To
                  JOCK.) I sent you to the A-ran islands,
                  you stupid bollocks.

                              JOCK
                  Do you think I'm stupid? You think I'd
                  believe you? You're strictly amateur
                  hour!! What are you talking about? You
                  couldn't send me a Christmas card!

                            MAGNANI
                  Alright . . . Gentlemen. I know what I
                  saw. Mr Quirk, I'm sorry, but your acting
                  leaves much to be desired. I didn't, and
                  I don't know how anybody else could,
                  believe you for a second. And this is
                  where we meet our problem, Mr
                  O'Malley. You . . . on the other hand . . .
                  were magnificent!

She hands him the flowers. O'MALLEY is flattered.

                            O'MALLEY
                  Well . . . Thank you. One tries . . . One
                  does what one . . .

He suddenly realises what her compliment entails. He goes pale.

                            O'MALLEY
                  Wait a minute. You don't think I . . . You
                  can't think I'd . . . Really . . . stagecraft,
                  you know . . . it's not like life . . .
                  I couldn't . . .

JOCK takes the flowers from him. They fall to the floor in slow motion.

                            O'MALLEY
                  Not the face.

134.   INT. HOTEL LOBBY NIGHT

We travel through the foyer of a posh Dublin hotel. Some people mill
about in tuxedos and ball gowns, drinking champagne.

135.   INT. HOTEL NIGHT

We sweep into a darkened Ballroom filled with tables, around which sit
the great and the good. There is a stage, behind which is a screen. An
awards ceremony is in progress. A pretty female MC in a ball gown
addresses the room. An ACTRESS has just accepted an award and is leaving
the stage to applause. At a table near the back sit TOM, O'MALLEY and
some of the cast of RICHARD III. They have finished their dinner, TOM
appears quite bored. O'MALLEY is covered in plaster. His leg is broken.
He's in a wheelchair. One arm is in a sling. He wears a neck brace and
has a black eye. He looks around at everyone, his eyes darting round the
room like he's trying to take a surreptitious shite in his seat.

                          MC
          And the award goes to . . . (Opening
          envelope.) This is stiff competition . . .

                      O'MALLEY
          Come on, you bitch . . .

                          MC
          . . . Anthony O'Malley . . .

                      O'MALLEY
                    (aggressively)
          Yes!!!

                          MC
          Richard the Third, Art of the State.

                      O'MALLEY
                    (like an animal)
          Yes! Yes! Yes! You losers. You stupid
          talentless bastards. Yes . . .

                          TOM
          I don't believe it . . .

O'MALLEY refuses help from an usher, and determinedly wheels himself
with one arm, bashing into tables.

                      O'MALLEY
                    (to the USHER)
          Fuck off. Fuck off.

He finally accepts the help of a pretty young woman.

                      O'MALLEY
          Thank you my dear.

On reaching the stage, he grabs the MC, somewhat inappropriately. She
grimaces weakly. and tries to get out of his embrace. A shoulder strap falls
away. O'MALLEY grips his award and approaches the microphone.

O'MALLEY

Best actor . . . Best actor . . . Acting . . .
What is it? What is acting? That's the
question I ask myself every night,
staring in the mirror, applying make-up,
watching myself slowly disappear as
I breathe life into whatever creation
I have to face and defeat over the next
three hours, before I can reclaim myself.

Never forgetting, all the while, theatre is
the temple where people come to
worship. And I never forget those
people. The little people, because
essentially, it's their story we're telling,
isn't it?

TOM looks on, aghast. BARRELLER calls out across the room, interrupting
the speech.

BARRELLER

It's on! It's on!

The GUESTS all look around in confusion as TOM and DOLORES join
BARRELLER, RONNIE, LESLEY, RITA, MARY, CLIVE, and crowd into the
bar. They are all looking up at a TV set.

136.   INT. BAR NIGHT

On the TV DOLORES is biting, into a sausage., She eats it like she's in
heaven. She holds up the packet.

DOLORES
(on TV)
McCullaghs! My God that's a right lump
of a sausage . . .

Everybody claps and cheers. DOLORES bows as they congratulate her.
O'MALLEY arrives but doesn't join in. He doesn't like her having the
limelight. He gives a forced frozen smile and wheels himself back into
the reception where the dancing is.

137.   INT. LATER AT A PARTY AFTER THE AWARDS NIGHT

We see an ACTRESS, a Judi Dench-type holding her award, being
congratulated by friends and being asked for her autograph.

PEOPLE are partying and dancing.

O'MALLEY'S sits ogling the women. He sits with BARRELLER, RONNIE,
and LESLIE.

                    BARRELLER
You were very lucky. There's not many
men can fall three storeys and live to
tell the tale.

                    O'MALLEY
An actor is always in peak condition,
Barreller.

                    BARRELLER
Oh, yeah, I suppose, right. (To RONNIE
beside him.) What kind of fuckin' eejit
just falls out a window?

                    RONNIE
What?

MARY comes and takes BARRELLER'S hand.

                    MARY
May I?

She leads BARRELLER to the dance floor.

                    MARY
You're going to have to pick me up.

                    BARRELLER
Oh, yeah, of course.

TOM and DOLORES are dancing.

                    TOM
Your dad doesn't suspect us, does he?

                    DOLORES
He just doesn't know what the fuck was
going on. He's just glad it's over. All the
agony.

She takes his hand and bends his thumb back, hurting him.

                    TOM
Hsss. Why do you do things like that?
Get over it, will you.

                    DOLORES
I like hurting you. Don't give me that.
You owe me, big time. I'll get over it. It's
just going to take some time, that's all.

She reaches for his thumb again, he pulls it away.

                    TOM
For fuck's sake!

She kisses him.

>   DOLORES
>   Is that better? Do you like that?

She makes a movement, touching her hair. TOM flinches. She laughs.

>   DOLORES
>   I'm not doing anything. Relax.

>   TOM
>   (clearly enjoying her)
>   I just don't know what's coming next,
>   you know?

>   DOLORES
>   Then I've got you just where I want you.

O'MALLEY tries wheeling himself onto the dance floor, someone tries to help him. He beats them off. His award is in his lap.

>   O'MALLEY
>   Fuck off! Fuck off! (Then, charmingly, to
>   a beautiful girl.) Hello

138. INT. THEATRE DAY

The set is now completely gone. MARY is alone on the stage.

>   MARY
>   Well that's our strange little story. I'm
>   like you. I can't believe we did all those
>   idiotic things either. But I pushed it
>   along. Because I'm a child – because
>   I can. But I'm getting older. That's
>   probably why I'm beginning not to
>   believe myself. I'm growing up. I'm
>   disappearing. Soon I'll be gone
>   altogether. Remember me.

The lights in the theatre are being switched off with a loud thunking sound.

THE END.

AFTERWORD

Afterword

A question I am always asked is, 'Which do you prefer working in, theatre or film?' I've always been slightly flummoxed. I have never been able to answer properly. I often say, 'Well, they're very different, but at the same time, they're sort of the same' or 'They are both more intense than each other,' or 'Well, when I'm making a film I long for the simplicity of a play and when I'm directing a play I wish I had the kind of resources films have . . . ' Obviously I should just say 'I don't know' but considering I make my living as a playwright, a screenwriter, a theatre director and a film director I can't say I don't know what the difference is between these jobs because I will just seem either (a) too arrogant to be bothered thinking about it or (b) a cretin.

But recently it's been dawning on me just what each discipline has to do with each other and what it is that makes them different. And it's not really about the camera or the money or the scale of a project. It's not about the glamour or the hard work or the hunger for recognition. It's not really about one being a purer form than the other. In my view the crucial similarities and differences between film and theatre are to do with the acting. Or, I should really say, the performances.

The other night an old friend of mine, an actor called Kevin Hely, called around to my house in Dublin. We sat around smoking cigarettes and speculating on what we had learned in the twelve years we've been doing this kind of thing. We reminisced about productions we'd been involved in, good and bad, down the years. We tried to remember what seemed important when we started and how we felt now. Worryingly, my views don't seem to have altered a whole lot. But Kevin's have. He has appeared in thirty-seven plays. Can you imagine what that must be like?

When he began acting the difference between him giving a good performance and a bad one seemed to him to be something beyond his control. Sometimes it felt great and sometimes it felt rubbish. And he could never figure out what had happened to make it so. He talked about trying to repeat the daily routine he practised on the days he gave a good performance. His reasoning was like this: 'God, my performance tonight was lousy. I was great on Monday night. Why was Monday better? I must try to do what I did on Monday again . . . '

If he got up at ten past nine on Monday morning, he got up at ten past nine every morning. If he ate one rasher and one sausage for his tea on Monday, that's what he ate every day. Of course any actor can tell you that these little routines have little or no effect on the actual work on stage. But it feels better. Life feels better. There are fewer surprises. You arrive at the theatre every night at the same time, seeing the same people, having had a similar day. The actor feels secure. But obviously the hardest part of the day is yet to come.

At about seven o'clock everything changes. Time seems to slide relentlessly towards the moment the actor has to walk out onstage and remember everything he or she has rehearsed. Many actors come to the theatre about an hour and a half before the curtain, just to hang out and get their mind and body into suitable condition. Actors develop little rituals among the company. They use lines from the play they are doing to make comments about their real life situations.

(You often hear surreal conversations in dressing rooms like

Actor A Oh God, I feel like Darren's wife in scene two. I've just put the biscuits in the wrong cupboard.

Actor B I know *exactly* what you mean . . .)

They may pair off or form little support groups to help each other with their lines, often doing a 'speed run' of the first twenty minutes of the show while they get changed in the dressing room. But quite often the actors, although glad to be working, may not like the production they are in.

Let's face it, just avoiding rejection is a great feat for many actors. The vast majority of them never get to choose their work. They have to go and audition for a director they may never have heard of, facing maddening competition from hundreds, possibly thousands of actors who want the same work. And once they get the part they spend the rest of the job being told what to do, sometimes not very politely, and if they refuse they are fired and replaced within hours. It strikes me that acting must be one of the worst jobs in the western world (having said that though I am a total pessimist when asked about how other people might be feeling . . .)

Then when they go and perform the show they are at the mercy of the critics. If the show doesn't get good reviews it's awful, if an actor is singled out for criticism it's the end of the world. It's also the end of the world if another actor is singled out for praise, especially if you have a similar-sized part.

And yet every actor in the world says they never read reviews. This isn't true. They all read reviews, if just indirectly. They have a great trick to protect themselves. They read them through other people. They will wait for someone to mention a review and then they'll say, 'I never read reviews. Was it a good one? Oh Really? What did it say?' All of this is totally natural. You have to protect yourself from being hurt or having your confidence destroyed (I always read reviews of my work. But I can't help it. I'm like some kind of sick animal when it comes to reviews. I hate it and yet I can't help it. I need to go to Review Readers Anonymous.)

Then there is the horror of the job ending and nothing else being on the horizon. And this isn't just fear of having no work, it's the fear of *never working again!* I'm not kidding. At the back of every actor's mind is the thought, 'Well, that's it. That was my last ever job as an actor. No one ever wants to work with me again. I can't continue like this . . .'

But of course they do continue. They have to. They love it too much. Acting is a brilliant thing to do. When you are in rehearsal you have to use so many aspects of your mind. You are trying to decide how a fictional character might behave if they were suddenly real. And human beings, fictional or not, are complex and whatever it is that makes us behave the way we do is mind-bogglingly complex. Simply the way a character enters a room may be a minefield of indecision for an actor. And it doesn't help working with a director they feel they can't trust. And sometimes they can rely too heavily on the director, which makes every tiny movement forward very difficult. But no matter what happens the relationships formed between actors in rehearsal are some of the most intense and spectacular you could ever hope to witness.

Coming into a rehearsal means you are not only exploring the emotions of a character but also your own emotions. In the course of deciding the trajectory of a scene the actors often exchange personal stories about themselves in a very short period of time. This is a great way to work, and also a great way to meet people. The bonds forged in rehearsal and performance can turn into bonds for life. As can, sadly, the little animosities. To bare one's inner feelings demands a great deal of trust and sometimes those of us who are less forthcoming may be seen as 'holding back' or 'being cold'. Sometimes an actor can be isolated in a company, becoming the scapegoat for the others' fears as to why something isn't working. The isolated actor is seen to be performing the play for all the wrong reasons (i.e. they are doing it as a job for money rather than working for the good of the team as they excavate the mysteries of the human soul). And so in this fragile world, is it any wonder that actors develop so many defences? David Mamet writes brilliantly about actors and their superstitions in his book *True and False*. He discusses all the displacement activity that goes on: 'I haven't found my character yet'; 'The audience were a bit slow tonight'; 'The energy levels weren't right'. There are a million excuses. And actors are no different to everyone else in this regard.

But what Kevin Hely says he has learned over the years is that in order to act properly all these fears must be faced and discarded. Only one person is responsible for the actor's performance on any given evening and that one person is the actor. This sounds painfully obvious, but like all simple things worth knowing it is hard won knowledge.

As a dedicated actor in the theatre Kevin and the company he works with in Dublin, meet every day, not just when they are rehearsing for a play, but *every day* at 9 am and start exercising. They do exercises in balance, agility, gymnastics, voice and so on. Just as dancers must attend class every day, and athletes must train, he believes that any performer must be in peak condition if they are to walk out in front of a paying crowd. The good actor performs his work simply and effectively and with a consistency that remains unwavering whether there are three people in the audience or three hundred. Thus Kevin is now on a different planet compared to where he was when he started out. Now he believes that he can't bother worrying about 'if the show felt a bit off tonight'. His feelings about the show are not important. He can only perform as best he can, as he has agreed to do it in rehearsal. Nothing 'magic' is supposed to happen on stage. He isn't waiting to be transformed or to get 'into character.' He simply does what he's supposed to do. He goes to the right places and says his lines with the force they need and with an inflection which we, the audience, can accept and believe. It sounds so simple, but when it's done properly it can blow your mind and leave you with a powerful memory to revisit for the rest of your life. Which brings me to the crucial difference between cinema and theatre as I know them.

An actor on screen has many attempts to get something right. Even if the actor and director aren't sure how something needs to be done they can shoot it a few different ways and decide later which is best. But the problem with this process for the actor, again, is one of choice. The actor in film has the illusion of choice. Unless the actor is a huge box-office draw and has enough clout to call the shots, the director always decides what gets used – never the actor. When a director is unhappy with the way an actor is performing in a scene, they can simply say, 'Alright we have that, and it's great, but just in case, let's do one a little less angry, just in case, you know, because that last one was, well wow, I don't want to say 'too much' but let's pull it back a little . . . ' and so on until the director, not the actor, is happy. Film is a director's territory. This is not to say that the situation is hopeless for the actor in a film. On the contrary, many actors have brilliant relationships with directors who they love working with again and again. They have developed a strong feeling of trust. But ultimately the actor must accept the fact that the director decides. An actor may feel that their best work is in a certain scene and the director may decide to cut the actor out or even cut the whole scene. With films being edited digitally now, it is so easy for the director to very quickly cut together tens of variations of a scene, (even on the set while shooting) and ultimately decide which suits the film as a whole. The actor has no say in this part of the storytelling process. What the actor must achieve in a film is getting each moment right. They move from moment to moment in no particular order which makes sense (most films are shot entirely out of sequence) and often without any time to rehearse properly. Ironically, film actors can work very quickly, just a couple of hours, to put a scene together in a film which then exists forever while theatre actors may work for months to achieve a performance which only lasts as long as the run of the show, usually a few weeks.

Of course a poor performance in a film can be made to look a lot better. With judicious editing and good music behind you, suddenly you can seem like an amazing star on the screen. But in the theatre there is simply nowhere to hide. If your performance is bad or just lazy you stick out like a sore thumb.

Ultimately the difference between making films and putting plays on is analogous to the band of musicians who go into the studio to record an album and the completely different world of performing the music live to an audience. The band can spend months perfecting their recording in the studio, and in a way edit it and shape it into a kind of coherence, just like a film. Mistakes are deleted. Only the best takes are used. But if you want to play live, you better be able to play well. Even though the music is available on a CD the fans want to see the music actually being performed. It's a great feeling to see a talented person perform live in front of you. Curiously the live experience both demystifies the performer and at the same time creates a whole other set of mysteries, i.e. 'How do they *do* that?'

The wonderful thing about films is that the resources at the director's disposal inflect the story for the audience. The director decides at every moment what the audience should look at, what they hear, and to a large extent how they feel. Some directors (e.g. Steven Spielberg) are notoriously manipulative of the audience's emotions, and this makes them popular just for that reason. Other directors are more reserved, they use the camera subtly to capture what it is they want us to see, allowing the audience the space to get it themselves (e.g. Woody Allen). They allow the acting to breathe. And that space which the actors are sometimes given is precisely what gives theatre its strength.

Theatre, as a much less inflected medium, really works when you are sitting in the audience and you realise that you are all feeling the same. The crowd laugh together, reassuring each other that it is okay to enjoy the experience. They respond as a group, each person having a subtly different but somehow unified experience. And when this is achieved simply by actors performing in front of us the very unmediated nature of the event lends it a power which is unsurpassed.

The sad truth though is that I can only really say I've had this kind of great theatre experience maybe four or five times in my life, whereas we've all seen lots of great films. It's so hard to achieve. First the play has to be brilliant. (It is nearly impossible to write a really good play, even most of the successful playwrights say only one or two of their plays are as good as they would have liked). Then it has to be performed well. And then the audience must be invested. The audience must want to enter the world of the play, because theatre is harder to see and hear than film. The characters appear smaller, their voices are distant. We are afraid we are missing something. If we get bored we feel trapped. It's hard to leave while the performance is underway because we don't want to disturb our neighbours or indeed the actors. The tickets are so expensive we get annoyed that we have been duped into paying for something that is not so good.

We don't feel so bad about watching a lousy movie. When we see a bad film we forget about it quickly. We moan a little bit but we say better luck next time, you know the conversation, 'Next week *I* pick what we see . . . '

But when we see a good theatre show we marvel at how, with so few resources, the performers took us on a journey into ourselves and out of ourselves. We are shocked. We know that there were no tricks. It wasn't 'fixed later.' It happened in front of us and it only worked because of the sheer force of the actors' talents. It's unquestionable. And it's why I am, and will continue to be, drawn back to the theatre.

Films are great. I love them. Who doesn't? As an art form they may be our greatest love. We always hold out hope of seeing another really good one soon. But plays are mysterious. I am convinced there is an awesome power in that simple communication. Barely inflected, hardly mediated – devastating.

And just like the musician who loves to go into the studio but also loves to crank up and play for the crowd on stage, I am a film maker and a playwright. And I love being both.

STILLS

Michael Caine as O'Malley and Dylan Moran as Tom

Abigail Iverson, as Mary, Tom's niece

Opposite page,top: Michael Caine as O'Malley
Bottom: Dylan Moran as Tom

Above: Ben Miller as the 'real' Clive
Below: Tom (Moran) as 'Clive'

Above: Lena Headey as Dolores. Below: Michael Gambon as Barreller

Above: Dolores (Headey) and 'Clive' (Moran)
Below: Tom (Moran) makes an unusual entrance to *Richard III*

Above: a further disguise – Tom, as 'Barreller' (Moran)
Below: 'Barreller' (Moran) with Jock (Michael McElhatton)

Above: Tom as 'Jock' (Moran)

Above: Dolores (Headey) and O'Malley (Caine)
Below: Mary (Iverson) and O'Malley (Caine)

Above: Michael Gambon as Barreller

Below: Barreller (Gambon) squares up to Jock (McElhatton)

Above: Tom (Moran) and Mary (Iverson) make an important call
Below: Jock (McElhatton) takes 'Clive' (Moran) for a ride

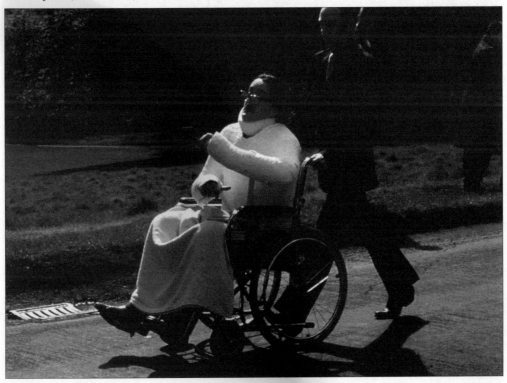

Above: Miranda Richardson as Mrs Magnani (with her hoods)
Below: Backstage, O'Malley (Caine) and Tom (Moran)

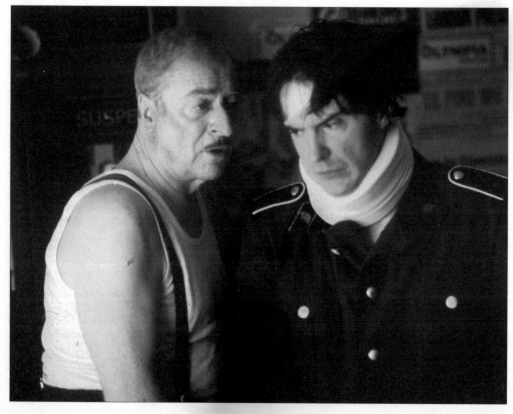

Above: onstage, O'Malley (Caine) as *Richard III*
Below: Conor McPherson, with Michael Caine and Dylan Moran on the set

CAST AND CREW CREDITS

FILMFOUR, MIRAMAX FILMS and SENATOR FILM
present in association with
BORD SCANNÁN NA HÉIREANN/THE IRISH FILM BOARD
a COMPANY OF WOLVES PRODUCTION
in association with FOUR PROVINCES FILMS
a CONOR McPHERSON FILM
starring MICHAEL CAINE and DYLAN MORAN

THE ACTORS

Also starring
MICHAEL GAMBON
LENA HEADEY
MIRANDA RICHARDSON
MICHAEL MCELHATTON
AISLING O'SULLIVAN
BEN MILLER
Introducing
ABIGAIL IVERSEN

Casting by	Susie Figgis
Make-Up and Hair Design	Veronica Brebner
Costume Designer	Consolata Boyle
Music by	Michael Nyman
Editor	Emer Reynolds
Production Designer	Mark Geraghty
Director of Photography	Seamus McGarvey B.S.C.
Associate Producers	Elinor Day, Romany Turner, John Erraught
Executive Producers	Paul Webster, Hanno Huth, Rod Stoneman
Story by	Neil Jordan
Producers	Stephen Woolley, Neil Jordan, Redmond Morris
Written and directed by	Conor McPherson

© Film Four Limited/Company of Wolves (The Actors) Ltd 2002

Cast (*in order of appearance*)

Mary . . . . .Abigail Iversen
Tom . . . . .Dylan Moran
Audition Director . . . . .Michael Colgan
Camcorder Girl . . . . .Deirdre Walsh
Stage Doorkeeper . . . . .Bill Hickey
Box Office Attendant . . . . .Veronica O'Reilly
Maurice (Usher) . . . . .Paul Ward
Dermot (Usher) .Brian McGuinness
O'Malley . . . . .Michael Caine
Actors in *Richard III* . . . . .Ian Fitzgibbon
. . . . .Brian McGrath
. . . . .Alison McKenna
. . . . .Annie Ryan
. . . . .Jude Sweeney
. . . . .Joanne Crawford
. . . . .Rachel Rath
Stage Manager .Deirdre O'Kane
Bookseller . . . . .Guy Carleton
Chief Fireman . . . . .Sean Tracey
Rita . . . . .Aisling O'Sullivan
Clive . . . . .Ben Miller
Barreller . . . . .Michael Gambon
Dolores . . . . .Lena Headey
Ronnie . . . . .Simon Delaney
Lesley . . . . .Alvaro Lucchesi
Jock . . . . .Michael McElhatton
Waiter . . . . .Damien O'Donnell
Mrs Magnani .Miranda Richardson
Magnani Hood 1 . . . . .Eamon Glancy
Magnani Hood 2 .Donagh Deeney
Alison Doody . . . . .Herself
Marty Whelan . . . . .Himself

Production Manager	Des Martin
1st Assistant Director	Peter Agnew
Sound Recordist	Simon Willis
Production Accountant	Wendy Ellerker
Additional Irish Casting	Rebecca Roper
Art Director	Ciara Gormley
Stand-by Art Director	Stephen Daly
Set Decorator	Johnny Byrne
Property Buyer	Jenny Oman
Draughtsman	Conor Devlin
Graphic Designer	Jenni Cooney
Scenic Artist	Laurence O'Toole
Art Department Trainee	Sinead Kavanagh
Focus Puller	Richie Donnelly
	Clapper Loader
	John Watters
Camera Grip	Malcolm Huse
Steadicam Operator	Paul Edwards
Camera Trainee	Cormac O'Máille
Video Assist	Clare McGrath
Additional Photography	Ciaran Barry
	Cian de Buitlear, Peter Robinson
Additional Camera Assistant	Shane O'Neill
Additional Camera Grip	John Dunne
Script Supervisor	Renée Foley Burke
Boom Operator	Conor O' Toole
Sound Trainee	Ian Johns
Production Coordinator	
	Anneliese O'Callaghan
Assistant Coordinator	Mary Gilroy
Production Trainee	Steven Davenport
Assistant to Mr McPherson & Mr.Morris	
	Miriam Cahill
Assistants to Mr.Woolley	
	Mariangela Angelucci
	Peter Ogunsalu
Assistant to Mr.Jordan	Cian McDonald
Assistant & Post Production Accountant	
	Clare Cunningham
Cashier	Mel Gallagher
Location Manager	Paddy McCarney
Assistant Location Manager	Edmund Sampson
Location Assistant	Evelyn O'Neill
2nd Assistant Director	Catherine Dunne
3rd Assistant Director	Sandra Corbally

Crowd Coordinator	Lisa Kelly
Trainee Assistant Directors	Sinead Murphy
	Andrew O'Malley, Bairbre Quinn
Production Assistant	Aoife Cassidy
Post Production Supervisor	Tricia Perrott
1st Assistant Editor	Gavin Buckley
2nd Assistant Editor	Janice Toomey
Conform Editor	Declan McGrath
Assistant Conform Editors	Mary Casey
	Sinead McGoldrick
	Anna-Maire O'Flanagan
Conform Trainees	Irina Maldea
	James Turpin
Rushes Trainee	Aidan O'Brien
Supervising Sound Editor	Douglas Murray
Dialogue Editor	Richard Quinn
Effects/Music Editor	Jon Stevenson
Assistant Sound Editor	Hugo Monks
Additional Assistant Sound Editor	
	Michael Lemass
Wardrobe Supervisor	Rhona McGuirke
Mr. Caine's Costumier	Jim Smith
Wardrobe Assistants	Ciara McArdle
	Lyndie MacIntyre
Assistant Costume Designer	
	Keelin O'Siochain
Key Cutter	Maggie Scobbie
Costume Trainee	Gaby Rooney
Make-Up Artist	Nuala Conway
Hairdresser	Conor McAllister
Trainee Make-Up Artist	Grainne Daly
Prosthetic Make-Up	
	Neil Gorton, Millennium FX
Supervising Gaffer	Lee Walters
Gaffer	Garret Baldwin
Electricians	Stephen Carthy
	Addo Gallagher, Dave Keogh
Generator Operator	Peter O'Toole
Stunt Coordinator	Donal O'Farrell
Stunt Performers	Phil Lonergan
	Geidrius Nagys
	Gary Robinson
	Laura Fox
	Alan Walsh
	Dominick Hewitt

Special Effects Coordinators . . .Pat Redmond
Brendan Byrne
Special Effects Crew . . . . .Aidan Byrne
Kevin Byrne, Paul Byrne, Gerry Farrell
P. J. Heraty, Kevin Kearns, Michael Kearns
Jimmy Lumsden
Prop Master . . . . .Eamonn O'Higgins
Chargehand Dressing Prop . . . . .Alan Dunne
Dressing Props . . . . .Daragh Lewis
Stand-by Props . . . . .Nuala McKernan
Dave Wallace
Props Storeman . . . . .Aran Byrne
Dressing Props Trainee . . .Jerome McDonnell
Construction Manager . . . . .Russ Bailey
Supervising Carpenter . . . . .Manus Daly
Chargehand Carpenter . . . . . . .Paul Keogh
Carpenters . . . . .Stephen Byrne
Thomas Barry Cunningham
Paschal Farrell
John Green
Owen McKenna
Tommy Rennick
Master Plasterer . . . . .Alan Cheevers
Master Painter . . . . .Edward Richardson
Owen Murnane
Painters . . . . .Daniel Lyons
Tony Murnane
William Richardson
Chargehand Rigger . . . . .Robert Reilly
Riggers . . . . .James Merrigan
Eoin Reilly
Chargehand Stagehand . . . . . .Anthony Kelly
Stagehands . . . . .Timothy Crimmins
Shane Donnelly
Stand-by Carpenter . . . . . . .David Oldman
Stand-by Painter . . . . .Garry O'Donnell
Stand-by Stagehand . . . . .Jimmy Gillen
Stand-by Rigger . . . . .Drew Meldon
Dialogue Coach . . . . .Gerry Grennell
Unit Nurse . . . . .Aine Doherty
Unit Publicity . . . . . .Freud Communications
Unit Publicist . . . . .Caitríona Ward
Stills Photographer . . . . .Tom Collins
Transport Captain . . . . .John Kavanagh

Action Vehicles Co-ordinator Stephen Carroll
Action Vehicles Assistant   . . .Dave Beakhurst
Mr.Caine's Driver . . . . .Terry O'Toole
Mr.McPherson's Driver . . . . .Pat Larkin
Unit Drivers . . . . .Matt Kelly
Frank Tobin
Facilities Drivers . . . . .John Douglas
Gerry Farrell, Michael Farrell
John Gallagher, Les Glasgow, David Jones
Padraig Kelly, Tony Lupton
George O'Dowd, Brian Thompson
Gerry Tulley, Breffni Winston
Facilities . . . . .Express Facilities
Winnebagos   Irish Film Location Facilities
Carleton Motor Homes
Location Facilities Ltd
Caterer . . . .Gerry Fitzsimmons, Cater Ireland
Re-Recording Mixers . . . . . .John Fitzgerald
Michelle Cunniffe
Sound Consultant . . . . . .Patrick Drummond
Foley Artists . . . . .Caoimhe Doyle
Andrea King
Foley Mixer . . . . .Michelle Cunniffe
ADR Recordist . . . . .Jean McGrath
Neil Conlon
Gerry Roche
Re-Recorded at . . . .Ardmore Sound, Ireland
Additional ADR recorded at
De Lane Lea, London
Goldcrest, London
Lime Street Sound, Dublin

Digital Visual Effects . . . .**Framestore CFC**
Executive Producer . . . . .Drew Jones
Compositing Artist . . . . .Gavin Toomey
Producers . . . . .Jo Nodwell
Anna Melly
Visual Effects Operators   Luke Drummond
Harriet MacMillan
Digital Lab Producer . . . .Alasdair MacCuish
Digital Lab Operator . . . . .Andy Burrow
Editorial . . . . .Tom Partridge

Company of Wolves

Business Affairs . . . . .Kate Wilson

FilmFour

Executive in Charge of Production:
Tracey Josephs
Business Affairs . . . . . . .Andrew Hildebrand
Helen Tulley
Production Finance: . . . . .Kim Ballard

Music Conducted by . . . . . .Michael Nyman
Violins . . . . .Gabrielle Lester
Catherine Thompson
Philippa Ibbitson
Viola . . . . .Catherine Musker
Cello . . . . .Anthony Hinnigan
Soprano/Alto Sax . . . . .David Roach
Simon Haram
Christian Forshaw
Baritone Sax, Alto Flute, Flute
Andrew Findon
Piano . . . . .Fender Rhodes
Synth . . . . .David Hartley
Piano . . . . .Michael Nyman
Double Bass/Bass Guitar . . . . . .Paul Morgan
Percussion . . . . .Martin Allen
Drums . . . . .Bob Knight
Voice . . . . .Fabienne Borget
Children's Choir
Moss Hall Junior School Choir
Children's Choir Coordinator Joan Lane, Wild
Thyme Productions
Orchestrator . . . . .Andrew Keenan
Orchestral Contractor . . . . . .Isobel Griffiths
Engineer . . . . .Austin Ince
Assistant Engineer . . . . .Alec Scannell
Ryu Kawashima
Paul Richardson
Music recorded at Abbey Road Studios, London
and Sony Music Studios, London
Mixed at . . . . .Snake Ranch, London
Published by . . . . . . .Chester Music Limited/
Michael Nyman Limited 2002
www.michaelnyman.com

Songs by Conor McPherson
and Fionnuala Ní Chiosáin

'Star of the Sea'
Lyrics and Music by Conor McPherson
Performed by Laura Cullinan,
Bébhinn Ní Chiosáin, Clíona Ní Chiosáin
and Niamh Reynolds
Recording courtesy of Company of Wolves
(UK) Ltd.
Published by Conor McPherson and Company
of Wolves (UK) Ltd.

'Waiting'
Lyrics by Conor McPherson,
Fionnuala Ní Chiosáin and Stephen Walshe
Music by Conor McPherson
Performed by Miranda Richardson
Recording courtesy of Company of Wolves
(UK) Ltd.
Published by Conor McPherson and Company
of Wolves (UK) Ltd.

'Come Back to Me'
Lyrics and music by Conor McPherson
and Fionnuala Ní Chiosáin
Performed by Fionnuala Ní Chiosáin
Recording courtesy of Company of Wolves
(UK) Ltd.
Published by Conor McPherson and Company
of Wolves (UK) Ltd.

'Could This be Love?'
Lyrics and music by Conor McPherson
Performed by Lena Headey and Dylan Moran
Recording courtesy of Company of Wolves
(UK) Ltd.
Published by Conor McPherson and Company
of Wolves (UK) Ltd.

'Úna's Waltz'
Music by Conor McPherson & Úna Ní
Chiosáin
Violin – Úna Ní Chiosáin
Recording courtesy of Company of Wolves
(UK) Ltd.
Published by Conor McPherson and Company
of Wolves (UK) Ltd

'Seems So Long'
Lyrics and music by Fionnuala Ní Chiosáin
Performed by Cathy Davey
Drums – Peter O'Kennedy
Recording courtesy of Company of Wolves
(UK) Ltd.
Published by Conor McPherson and Company
of Wolves (UK) Ltd.

'Ce Beau Matin'
Music by Michael Nyman
Lyrics by Conor McPherson
and Fionnuala Ní Chiosáin
Perfomed by Fabienne Borget
and The Michael Nyman Band
Recording courtesy of Company of Wolves
(UK) Ltd.
Published by Chester Music Ltd./
Michael Nyman Ltd., Conor McPherson
and Company of Wolves (UK) Ltd.

'Lovely Morning'
Lyrics by Conor McPherson
and Fionnuala Ní Chiosáin
Performed by Cathy Davey
French horn – Niall Ó Ciosáin,
Violin – Úna Ní Chiosáin
Drums – Peter Kennedy
Recording courtesy of Company of Wolves
(UK) Ltd.
Published by Conor McPherson and Company
of Wolves (UK) Ltd.

Songs Recorded at . . . . . . .Area 51, Dublin
Produced, Programmed & Engineered by . . .
Ken McHugh
French Translation
Éamon Ó Ciosáin and Gwénaelle L'Azou
Cameras supplied by . . . . .Panavision Ireland
Stills Processing . . . . .Blow Up Stills Lab
Lab Contact . . . . .John Ensby
Colour Grader . . . . .Martin Walsh
Telecine Services . . . . . .Technicolor Imaging
Editing Equipment London Editing Machines
Post Production Services
Windmill Lane Pictures

Negcutters Professional Negative Cutting Ltd.
Titles & Opticals . . . . .Cineimage
Post Production Script . . . . . .Sapex Scripts
Travel Agent . . . . .Flair Travel
Copyright Clearance
Bellwood Communications
Completion Bond . . .Film Finances UK Ltd.
Insurance Services . . .AON/Albert G. Ruben
Legal Services . . .Matheson Ormsby Prentice,
James Hickey, Ruth Hunter Olswangs,
Susan Waddell, Lisbeth Savill
S J Berwin – Nora Mullally
Auditors . . . . .Ernst & Young
U.K. Auditors . . . . .Malde & Co
Banking Services . . . . .Anglo-Irish Bank
. . . . .Bank of Ireland
. . . . .HSBC, UK

Extracts from
'You and Me Tide'
(dir: Conor Morrissey)
Courtesy of Bord Scannán na hÉireann/
Irish Film Board

'Je t'aime John Wayne'
(dir: Toby McDonald)
Courtesy of Luke Morris & Toby McDonald

Special Thanks to:
Paddy Breathnach
Tom Debenham
Arlen Figgis
Drew Jones
Nick Marston
Mark Nelmes
William Sergeant
Jeffrey Katzenberg, Walter Parkes,
Laurie MacDonald, Paul Lister,
Laura Fox, Ronni Coulter
Department of Defence
Dublin City Council

Produced with the support of investment
incentives for the Irish Film Industry provided
by the Government of Ireland

Filmed on location in Dublin, Ireland